Do You Know Yourself?

Do You Know Yourself?

Archimandrite Symeon Kragiopoulos

translated by Monk Cosmas (Shartz)
with the assistance of Petros Xides

Divine Ascent Press
Manton, California
2010

Do You Know Yourself?
English translation © 2010 from the 3rd Greek edition by Divine Ascent Press

ISBN: 978-0-9714139-5-5
Published by Divine Ascent Press
PO Box 439
21770 Ponderosa Way
Manton, CA 96059
www.divineascent.org

Divine Ascent Press is the publishing arm of the
Monastery of St. John of Shanghai and San Francisco
www.monasteryofstjohn.org

All rights reserved. No part of this book may be reproduced or transmitted in any form or by any means, electronic or mechanical, including photocopying, recording, or by any information storage and retrieval system without written permission from Divine Ascent Press.

Originally published Greek as Γνωρίζεις τόν ἑαυτό σου; © Monastery "Τό Γενέσιον τῆς Θεοτόκου" 2000; 2nd ed. 2003; 3rd ed. 2008.

The Scripture quotations contained herein are from the Revised Standard Version Bible, copyright © 1946-52, 1971, by the Division of Christian Education of the National Council of Churches of Christ in the U. S. A., and are used by permission. All rights reserved.

PRINTED AND BOUND IN THE UNITED STATES OF AMERICA BY VERSA PRESS, INC.

Contents

Editorial Introduction to the English Edition vii
Translator's Introduction xi

Chapter One: A Theological Approach to Conflicts

    A Dive into Ourselves 3
    The Position of the Soul Before Any Sort of Reality 12
    Blocked in Spite of our Efforts 19
    "That They May Be One in Us" 24

Chapter Two: Moving Toward People

    Attachment to Others 33
    Unhealthy Compliance 40
    Submission Which Doesn't Liberate 49
    Love as an Unwholesome Expression 57

Chapter Three: Moving Against People

    Those Who Consider Others Their Enemies 67

Chapter Four: Moving Away from People

    Healthy and Unhealthy Solitude 75
    Why Does One Close Oneself up
        in an Unhealthy Way? 87
    Far from Themselves 92
    Closed off in a Compulsive Way 98
    The Type that Moves within Negativity 104
    Unpleasant Consequences of Opening
        up to Others 107

Chapter Five: The Idealized Image

    Identifying with a Fantasy 115
    The Idealized Image and Pride 122
    The Disintegration of the Person.................... 126
    Unfavorable Influences of Contemporary Society 132
    The Idealized Image Replaces Ideals 138
    The Idealized Image: Our Imaginary Self 145
    Are We Serving an Idol? 149
    The Idealized Image Must Die 157
    The Externalization of the Idealized Image.............. 167
    Self-Loathing..................................... 176

In place of an epilogue 183

Editorial Introduction to the English Edition

This book, entitled *Do You Know Yourself?*—which could have been subtitled *A Truer Approach to our Deeper Self* – is comprised of a series of talks[1] which took place between October 1970 and May 1972 in the auditorium of the Holy Metropolis of Thessaloniki, given by Archimandrite Symeon Kragiopoulos.

From the time of his ordination in 1954 until the present day, Fr. Symeon has been working as a lecturer and spiritual advisor in the Metropolis of Thessaloniki. Specifically, beginning in 1974, the base of his spiritual work has been Panorama (a suburb of Thessaloniki), where, over the course of the years, he has created two monastic communities, a brotherhood of monks and a sisterhood of nuns, of which he is the head. During these years he has made frequent trips to other Metropolises inside and outside Greece for his work as a lecturer and spiritual advisor. Whenever he lectures he tries to make himself available to be enlightened by God and as a result what he tells today's Christians is what the Spirit of God would like to say to us. The subjects of his lectures— of a great variety – are always spiritual. Along with the spiritual and theological approach, the psychological aspect is also very characteristic of the subjects covered in his talks. And this is because he has ascertained, from his experience as a spiritual advisor, that in order for a soul to have the potential to engage in spiritual matters and subsequently to

---

1   The talks were not transcribed by the speaker. They were spoken at that time before an audience. When it was a matter of turning them into a book, they were taken from the tape and then the appropriate [editorial] work took place (by members of the sisterhood) so that certain elements of the spoken word which did not stand up well in the written text could be smoothed out.

be able to live a spiritual life, it first has to find its psychological equilibrium.

The talks included in the present edition were based on the book *Our Inner Conflicts*[2] by Karen Horney (1885-1952), who worked as a psychoanalyst in Germany and later in America.

We know that in the twentieth century great psychologists appeared who laid the foundations for what is called the psychology of the unconscious or depth psychology. This is "a new direction in psychology, which is distinguished from the directions taken previously in that it intends to penetrate the deepest level of psychic experiences, the level which is posited as existing below conscious experiences."[3]

In her books, Karen Horney challenged quite a few of the important principles of psychoanalytic theory as formulated by Freud – who, as we know, is considered the founder of psychoanalysis—and asserted that neuroses are caused by disturbances in a person's relationships with others.[4]

The present book is made up of twenty-five talks, which we have divided into five chapters. In the first chapter, by taking a theological approach to conflicts, the speaker explains the role of psychology in the spiritual life. On account of sin, more or less all of us are blocked by various forms of unhealthy conditions which come from the incorrect position we take before the one and only reality, which is God, and subsequently before other people, with whom

---

2   New York, London: W. W. Norton, 1945. [Note: For the convenience of the English-language reader, footnote references in the Greek edition to Greek-language sources have wherever possible been replaced by the equivalent readily available reference works in English. tr.]
3   Encyclopedic lexicon *Iliou*, vol. 18, p. 845.
4   See article "Unconscious" in *The New Encyclopaedia Britannica Micropaedia* vol. 12, p. 125.

we make up a single humanity. Karen Horney considers that "all the blockages of a person, all the mixed-up things, are due or have in any case a relationship with one of the three movements which a person can make in relation to other persons." And this is because a person cannot stand and cannot exist as a monad. To be sure, at the root of our existence there are also others. In the final analysis this means that one cannot disregard the existence of others.

The second chapter explains for us the movement toward people. When a certain person cannot stand psychologically on his own two feet, he feels the need to rely on something. And so he can be led to an attachment to others, to a slavish dependence on others, to an unhealthy compliance toward others (a child toward its mother, a wife toward her husband, a spiritual son toward his spiritual father).

In the third chapter he analyzes the movement against people. The tendency in certain people is to dominate and even become sadistic without much hesitation. The basis of this movement of persons is egoism.

Many people in contemporary society – and maybe we ourselves could be counted among them without knowing it—are isolated, alienated from others and closed in on themselves in an unhealthy way. The reason is individualism, which means a lack of genuine love and communion with others, as is made clear by the title of the fourth chapter, "Moving Against People."

What we all suffer from, however, as the fifth chapter tells us, is the idealized image. A person has the tendency to fashion an imaginary – usually favorable – image of himself, which leads him away from reality and renders him disorganized. A person ends up becoming a victim of this condition as he reduces himself the point of serving an idol – the idealized image which he has about himself – and he cannot live spiritually.

We believe that if we view these positions of Karen Horney within the framework of Orthodox spirituality and theology, they still hold good for our time, because they make known and confirm certain truths about human beings which have, as we would put it, a perennial character, given the fact that no matter how much time passes, human beings in essence remain the same. In this sense the redemptive message of the Gospel is timely for the human being of every period, as also are the things said by the Fathers of the Church and particularly the neptic Fathers. We should note here that the truths spoken by Karen Horney and some of the other psychologists have already been said by the Fathers of our Church and particularly by the neptic Fathers.

The lecturer did not attempt to approach the subject of man's inner conflicts simply from a psychological viewpoint alone, but rather went further and deeper into it theologically and spiritually. In this way, we believe that the reader who studies these talks will be helped to learn about himself more than he knows already and will acquire a truer communion with God and other human beings, and in so doing he will be able to stand on a firm footing in life and be made worthy to respond to the purpose for which he exists, which is none other than salvation and redemption.

Translator's Introduction

This book is the first to be made available in English translation from the thirty books published in Greece based on Fr. Symeon's lectures and homilies. It is part of a four-part series on psychological problems and the spiritual life.

In producing this translation we have striven to balance a number of factors. One of our foremost aims has been to preserve both the meaning and the "feel" of Fr. Symeon's lectures which formed the basis for the Greek text of this book, and yet at the same time to bear in mind that the readers have in their hands a written text and not merely a transcription of the spoken word. We also have consistently endeavored to balance considerations of accuracy with an avoidance of the sort of fussy literalism which would undermine the impression of a spoken and almost conversational style. We have always tried to arrive at a style in English which would serve as a plausible representation of the style of the lectures as delivered in Greek. In certain spots, with the agreement of the Sisterhood of the Holy Monastery of the Nativity of the Theotokos (the editors and publishers of the Greek text), we have silently modified certain words and phrases which have a connection with the oral delivery of the talks, and have brought them a little more into conformity with a written style. These include modifications in references such as "two weeks ago, when we had our last meeting here" or "last Sunday."

The effort to render an appropriate style was complicated by the fact that Fr. Symeon drew many of the concepts presented in this book from a book by the psychiatrist Karen Horney, *Our Inner Conflicts*, which he read in Greek translation but which Horney, a native speaker of German, wrote in English not long after arriving in the United States.

We brought the same strategy of balance between accuracy and smooth English to this aspect of the translation as well, so that for the most part Fr. Symeon's technical vocabulary which clearly derives from Horney's book is rendered by the terms she herself uses, except in a few selected cases where her choice of words seemed somewhat unidiomatic. For example, she uses the term "trend" (toward a certain type of behavior) and we have replaced it by "tendency" as being a more common way of expressing the same idea in a rather colloquial style such as that of Fr. Symeon's lectures.

Three additional points call for special remark. Gender-inclusive language has come to be an issue in English prose, and as a result we have attempted to render passages in which the masculine in Greek is used indifferently to refer to men or women by a variety of strategies in English. Our aim in each instance has been to meet the requirements of modern English prose style as unobtrusively as possible.

Second, as is standard in producing an edition of a book in translation, we have replaced the footnote references to Greek-language sources with references to easily available English-language sources. For example, where the editors of the Greek text have included volume and page references to an edition of one of the Church Fathers published by a Greek publishing house, we have offered the equivalent reference (with page number) to an English translation of the same work.

Third, the editors of the Greek edition have taken short passages from Fr. Symeon's text and placed them at empty portions of pages at the ends of chapters or on otherwise blank pages. These passages are not always verbatim citations from the text, but are sometimes slightly adapted in order to be able to stand on their own. The editors of the Greek text inform us that the main function of these extracts is typographical—that is, to enhance the visual presentation of the book. We have followed suit, but our placement of these extracts does not correspond in every case to that of the Greek text, since our placement of them, like that of the Greek editors, is determined by considerations of layout.

Fr. Cosmas (Shartz) is a monk at the Monastery of St. John of Shanghai and San Francisco in Manton, California, where he translates, edits, and proofreads for Divine Ascent Press.

Petros Xides was born in Greece and migrated to the United States in 1977. He is a spiritual son of Fr. Symeon. In his spare time, he teaches Greek to adults and children at Resurrection Greek Orthodox Church in Castro Valley, California.

Chapter One

A Theological Approach to Conflicts

A Dive into Ourselves

With God's help and with the help of certain things we know we'll try to make a dive into our soul. Let's offer an example. We see a lake. The water appears calm or perhaps there's a little movement, but nobody knows what's deep within it. However, when someone who is trained in such things – a frogman, for example – plunges in and goes a meter below the surface, two meters, three meters, he goes to the bottom of the lake provided that it isn't extremely deep, and he sees what's down there and informs us. And sometimes we take actions in keeping with what he tells us.

We'll try, then, to make a venture of that sort below the surface, a dive of that sort into the depths of our existence, in order to correct certain conditions that exist there that create troubles not only in us ourselves but also in our relations with other people.

Conscious, Subconscious, Unconscious

Remember what we said earlier – that according to contemporary psychology man's psyche is composed of the three levels of conscious, subconscious, and unconscious.

In the conscious the person has all those things he understands, perceives, feels, and he can control. I have this, that, and the other thing. I feel this way, I feel another way. Below the conscious is the subconscious, and below the subconscious is the unconscious. Within the subconscious and the unconscious there is a great deal of content, and this content is unknown. The person isn't aware of it.

In the past, we've mentioned that according to psychologists one-tenth of the person is conscious and nine-tenths is subconscious and unconscious. Allow me to mention again the example I used at that time so that we can understand this. Imagine a watermelon in the middle of a lake, in the middle of a cistern or a tank full of water. The watermelon is floating on the water. And let's suppose that the part of the watermelon that's out of the water is one-tenth and the other nine-tenths is in the water. One-tenth appears. Nine-tenths doesn't appear.

If we translate this to man's psyche, let's suppose that the whole content of the person's psyche is ten-tenths, we'll say that by analogy only one-tenth of the psyche is conscious. This is what we see, what we know and control. This means that nine-tenths of our self is unknown. One part, perhaps three-tenths, is subconscious, that is, it's a little below the level of the conscious, and we get an idea of what's happening there. Six-tenths, however, is unconscious, it's a dark basement, and we're completely unaware of it. And it's not merely unknown. Inside there are a thousand and one tendencies, some this way and others that way, and which inside in the depth of our existence create conflicts and battles and try to destroy one another. That is, one tendency tries to annihilate the other.

While we don't know all these things – since they're in the depth of our existence, in that dark part that doesn't appear – while they're unseen, non-appearing, nevertheless we live them, because they're within our self. They aren't something outside of our self. And often it's precisely these hidden things within us that lead us hither and yon. They cause us to speak this way or that, to conduct ourselves in one manner or another, to take this or that position.

We spoke previously[1] about that mother who, when her child is writing, pays no attention to the good letter, but to

---

[1] In the first part of the gathering the subject of the talk was "Parents and children."

the badly written or crooked letter, and points it out to her child. She thinks that when she acts like this she's doing an important job at that point. We say this because we have to emphasize that this mother believes that she's helping her son, that she's working and struggling for her son's good. This is what she believes, this is what she thinks, and that's why she acts this way. Deep down, however, there's something else she doesn't know. But whether she knows it or not, it exists, and this is exactly what impels her to see the crooked G rather than the good O, to see the spelling mistakes rather than seeing what's correct where it exists. There is, then, something deep in her psyche that acts without her knowing it, and which impels her in this direction or that. In general in every man there is this part of his existence—which is in fact the larger part—which is unseen, unknown, and which leads man hither and yon.

"The heart is deep beyond all things"

Of course holy scripture said this long ago. As we read in the book of the prophet Jeremiah, "The heart is deep beyond all things."[2] That is, man's heart has a depth, and however far one proceeds inside oneself, however much one understands, or however much one knows oneself, there is still a part that will remain unknown.

And we see that later the Fathers of the Church do everything they can to know themselves. That is, they try to go ever deeper into their souls so that the part of the soul that is unknown becomes known one day and is continuously baptized in God's grace, so that God's grace continuously influences it, illumines it, and sanctifies it. That's why a

---

[2] Jeremiah 17: 9 "The heart is deep beyond all things, and it is the man. Even so, who can know him?"

reborn man, a holy man, isn't led about by inner conditions of which he's unaware. One would say that "he's led about" knowingly and consciously. That is, he knows what he's doing, he knows what he's seeking. And in the final analysis, he's led by God's grace, which has permeated to the depths of his existence. It has permeated his soul to the very depths.

Freud, Jung, Adler, Horney

As you know, up until a few decades ago, what are called the unconscious and the subconscious were unknown from the scientific viewpoint, from the psychological viewpoint. The Church Fathers were not unaware of them, however, nor is Holy Scripture. The Fathers said what they had to say on this subject and did what they did and were sanctified. Science, however – psychology, pedagogy – was unaware of the reality of the unconscious and the subconscious.

A few decades ago, however, there appeared some great psychologists who occupied themselves particularly with this effort to make deeper progress into man's psyche, to explain certain of man's actions. Why is it, for example, that a man acts this way or another way? Why does he behave like this without understanding that what he's doing isn't correct? He doesn't understand – which means that he's led hither and yon by something.

So then, as we said, while the Fathers knew these things, a few years ago, in some way science discovered the subconscious and the unconscious. And psychoanalysis began to be practiced, and a lot has been said about it, and today it's practiced in all the countries of Europe. Even here in Greece there are certain expert psychoanalysts who try, with the method of psychoanalysis, to help men who are suffering and afflicted.

The point is that whatever a man does, if he does it apart from God, in the final analysis even the good that he decides to do is not as effective as it could be if it happened by God's grace, and often instead of bringing good, it does harm.

The first to appear was Freud, certainly who said some correct things, some true things, but he also said all those strange things on the subject of psychology as well as many erroneous, blasphemous, and sinful things. Adler and Jung, who were Freud's disciples, quickly understood that their teacher didn't get everything right and at a certain point they disagreed with him and both abandoned him. Adler followed his own line of thinking and carved out a new path on these psychological themes. Jung, on the other hand, also followed out his own line of thinking. Perhaps he made further progress and had more good things to say than the other two, but he, too, was led astray.

Like all men—and let's keep it in mind—we, too, can be led astray, even when we're doing the most holy things. It's not simply those who occupy themselves with science and conduct experiments and research who can be led astray, but we, too, who occupy ourselves with the holiest things, with the most spiritual matters, and we should know that as men we will make mistakes, as men it will happen that we are led astray. The reason, for example, that in Greece today, while there are many of us who have some interest in spirituality and are trying to do something, in the end we have made a mess of it and flounder about—that is, we haven't discovered ourselves yet so as to begin doing something little by little— is that each of us thinks that what he's doing is perfect and everyone must follow it, everyone must accept it. The truth, however, is that every act, whatever it is, insofar as we men do it, however much God's grace may be there somewhere, in the final analysis it has a human seal to it. And if we think that this human seal is the divine seal, then from that point on the act ceases to be spiritual, and instead of good it causes harm.

Since, therefore, those who occupy themselves with divine matters can fall into error as human beings, so much the more can those men. And so Freud, Adler, and even Jung were led astray.

I recall that when I was reading Jung's views on these psychological topics, some of his positions were unconvincing to me. "It's all good," I thought, "but I feel this point here isn't correct." That was what occurred to me to say. Some of his positions, that is, weren't in agreement with what the Fathers say, with what Holy Scripture says, with what the whole spirit of Christianity presupposes.

Not long ago – about a year ago – a book fell into my hands which was written by a psychiatrist and psychoanalyst named Karen Horney, who appears to be a very great and important psychiatrist and she provided a great service, as it seems, there in America—she's dead now—and she herself spent time as a disciple of Freud. It impressed me that she didn't accept what Freud says, that is, his basic theses, which caused such harm in the world and in psychology itself. Furthermore I was impressed by what she said about Jung. "Whereas Jung," she writes, "says this at this point, I don't agree and it's more correct to take it this way," and she indicates her own position.

As I was reading her book, then, I kept seeing that she didn't agree with certain of Jung's theses. Jung is considered to be a religious man – certainly he was a Protestant—and quite often he says that rather than visiting psychiatrists, it would be better for men to visit priests, that is, confessors, spiritual fathers. But since priests aren't trained, he says, that's why people have recourse to psychiatrists.

Jung has good things to say, but as I told you, certain of his positions were unconvincing to me as well. And I noticed that her position convinced me more, unlike Jung's, which left certain questions within me.

The facts of psychology in the spirit of the Church Fathers

Since we haven't undertaken specialized studies on these topics and we can't be absolutely certain about them, nor do we have time to occupy ourselves with them in detail, nor perhaps do we have the qualifications—because one must have the appropriate qualifications—we can't somehow create our own school, our own method and theory and say things of our own. We'll take the good things, the sound things, from what the experts say. We'll take them as one takes facts from medical science, because you must know that certain of the things psychology or psychiatry says are rather like what medicine in general says. Doctors study what sick people display, they do certain experiments, and they arrive at certain conclusions. And they say, for example, for this pain to go away, you must take aspirin. For this illness to go away, you must have surgery. Or, you feel a pain here, but the trouble isn't here, it's in your stomach. And provided that they've carried out specialized studies and have learned things and know them, we're obligated to accept those things. The only difference is that we'll look at all these things in the spirit of the Gospel, in the spirit of the Fathers, in the spirit, generally speaking, of Christianity and the revelation.

It's the same here. After research, after hard work, psychology has made some observations today, some discoveries, and has drawn certain conclusions. Certainly the

Fathers knew these things, as it has been said, from another point of view and in another manner. It's not permissible for us now—at least this is my humble opinion and I don't know whether I'll change my mind later – to cross them out with the stroke of a pen and say, "Forget about them. Let them say what they want" if in certain questions they can be helpful to us.

We can't say that the doctor can't help us. Even an ascetic, who may be the greatest saint, if he has a stomachache, yes, he'll be courageous, he'll be patient, but if he sees that God doesn't cure him, he'll go to the doctors. We have in mind the holiest men of the Holy Mountain, who come to Thessaloniki and have operations or undergo treatments to be healed. God could heal them, but it's as if He told them, "Since there's a way for you to be healed by the doctors, I'm not healing you. You'll go there and be healed."

It's the same thing in the situation that lies before us. As long as there are illnesses today that are related to psychology, that are related to these psychological investigations, and as long as we have the facts that come from these discoveries, if I may put it in this way, why shouldn't we use them? It's not permissible for us to cross all those things out with the stroke of a pen and say, "We don't accept them." We shall accept them. The only difference is that we shall see these things in the spirit of the Fathers, in particular the spirit of the Neptic Fathers, who help us a great deal in this sector. It was certainly in another way that the Fathers saw these points, understood them, confronted them, and finally conquered them, overcame them and became sanctified.

Today science comes along and discovers all these things in another way. But the bad thing about science is that it sees things in a dry, merely scientific manner, and in the end, when specialists, mere scientists, try to help the men who have recourse to them, it's not infrequent – from what I know, and I have some experience in these matters – that instead they make them worse.

On the other hand, when one uses these things in the spirit of Christ, in the spirit of the Gospel, in the spirit of the Gospel and the Fathers, they are useful and help us a great deal. Because in and of themselves these things are true.

With the goal to truly live

With all of this I want to say, brethren, that with the help of the facts of psychology, with the help of the spirit of the Fathers, we'll make an effort to enter a little deeper within ourselves, to know ourselves. We'll try to make a deep dive into ourselves.

And you know what? We'll escape from a great many ugly things. That is, if God helps us and we catch those "fish" that dance around within us and do so much harm, we'll escape from a great many sufferings. And our life will be easier, freer, and those of us who truly want to live the spiritual life will really be able to live it. Because—and I have to say this—someone who has complications within him, who has been blocked internally by any such things, can't live the spiritual life. He certainly won't be lost. If he takes heart, if he's patient and says, "I have these problems. What am I to do? Since I'm not getting to the bottom of this, I hope God will save me," and if he passes away with this patience and with this hope, God will save him, except that he won't be able to live out his spiritual progress in this place. But I wonder if this kind of man can have that patience. Because these are the sort of things that create such darkness and carry a man away to such a degree that they don't allow him to hope in God, to trust in God so as to calm down, to be at peace, to taste a little of God's grace.

The Position of the Soul Before Any Sort of Reality

A bad thing, and another, worse than the first

Whether we recognize it or not, in the final analysis each of us is the victim of an inner condition which is something like a labyrinth. He's a victim of a thousand and one elements existing within him. We're led about by different life-altering experiences,[1] by a lot of situations which act without much consideration of us, without being under the control of our personality, under our conscious control. And while we're victims, while we're led about by all these dark things, we're unaware of it.

It's a bad thing, certainly, a very bad thing, that we're victims. We're in the image of God, created by God very good,[2] created uncomplicated and not complex and with labyrinths—and for us to live in such a condition! That's bad. But what's worse is when we don't know what's happening to us, when we don't know what's going on with us. That is, while we're led about by this or the other ugly condition, while we're victims of this or the other experience, we take this condition and this experience for something good, we take it for the treasure of our soul, for the treasure of our existence.

These conditions are expressed towards others as well, and of course, since they are bad in themselves, they are therefore

---

[1] Fr. Symeon uses a term here and elsewhere in this book, βιώματα, which carries the meaning of "that which collectively and subconsciously remains in the soul from certain life experiences, and controls to a certain degree emotions, ideas, and behavior." It will be rendered as "life-altering experiences," "life-experiences," or simply "experiences" depending on the context. [tr.]
[2] See Genesis 1:31.

expressed in a bad way and cause harm. We, however, are convinced that we act so correctly, more so than anyone else and ever so much more correctly than we ourselves have ever acted before. And this, I repeat, is the worst thing.

And if you like, let's translate this to the spiritual sphere as well. As the Fathers say, the bad thing isn't merely that we're sinners. God knows that. The great harm comes if we don't recognize this condition of sinfulness in us, and if what needs to happen for us to be released from it doesn't happen. And more specifically, if we don't go to Him Who heals man from sin. Consequently the bad thing isn't just that we're sinners, but also that we don't go to the Healer, we don't go to the Savior, to the Redeemer.

It's a bad thing, then, that the depth of our existence is like a labyrinth, where there are these dark autonomous forces that sometimes come into collision with one another, shoving one another—and one would say that they act in such a way that it's as if they want to annihilate one another—and at other times they emerge to harm others, although at that time we think we're offering service to others, that we're becoming their benefactors. In a basic sense we too are victims of our own dark forces, and others, also, will become victims of them. But it isn't just that. It's also a bad thing when someone has no suspicion at all that something isn't going well inside him and he doesn't look to see exactly what's happening, what's not going well and how it can be confronted.

Evil is foreign to our nature

I'd like to repeat once again what we've said on other previous occasions: These things that create this labyrinth, these dark forces, these conditions that are so ugly—they work in such a way that they don't let us see them. They are kneaded into our existence to such a degree, they are kneaded into the natural condition of our soul to such a degree and are so united with our being that we think these conditions are us, while they are completely foreign to our nature. They are foreign in the sense that they are not of the nature of our soul.

These psychopathological conditions, these dark conditions that are the results of the fall, of sin, lack a foundation. After all, who created them? God didn't create conditions of that sort. Behind everything is God. God is He from Whom all things originate. But God created only good things. Ugly things are all consequences of the fall. That's also why – no matter how much these things exist inside us – they are outside our nature.[3]

And as I was saying before[4] – we'll provide a better explanation in our next talk – we act quite inappropriately when we don't keep this in mind in our relationship even with little children. Let's say that we discover a shortcoming in a child, for example, that he cries, and instead of saying that this child is overcome by crying, we say that "he's a crybaby." That is, we put a label on him and in this way we unite the shortcoming with the child's very existence. Or way say, "he's a liar," "he's a fraidy-cat" or something similar. This is a very bad thing.

We don't do this only to children but also to ourselves. That is, we often view these unseen forces, these sinful forces, these forces of psychological nature, as very much united with our existence, with our being, and especially

---

3 "That God is not the cause of evils." See St. John of Damascus, *Exposition of the Orthodox Faith*. Book III, ch. xiv, "Concerning the volitions and free-wills of our Lord Jesus Christ." vol. 9, pp. 57-60 in *Nicene and Post-Nicene Fathers* series. Peabody, MA: Hendrickson Publishers, 1995.

4 See footnote 1 on p. 3.

to such a degree that we identify them with our being. We can't separate them. That is, we can't see our existence as very good, see that it emerged good from God's hands, that it's in the image of God. We can't see that even though these ugly things came along and fastened onto our existence, got tangled up with our existence, they don't cease as substance to be foreign to our existence, to be results of the fall. And precisely because this identification takes place, because this "blending" occurs—as if we had a mixture much like when we put flour and water together and make dough, and from that point on the flour and water don't separate but they're dough, or as when the chemist mixes up two chemical substances and they become one mixture—because therefore our soul and all these negative things become one mixture, or we feel they are like a mixture and we can't distinguish our soul as something that came out good—very good—from God, that's why we can't see that we do have all these negative elements.

Here's the big mistake, the great evil, that I mentioned. We each have this or the other. Okay, we have it. This, however, isn't the great evil. The great evil is when one doesn't understand that he has these things and he doesn't do what he's supposed to do to be delivered from them.

And that is why we're discussing them here, and discussing them elsewhere and privately with those of course who think that such matters must be discussed. Perhaps it could be that we'll be helped in this way so as to be able fearlessly and without prejudice to see the reality that exists within us, and also so as not to hesitate to do what we must do—whatever sacrifice is required of us—to be freed as much as possible from these foreign forces, from these foreign elements, from these cancers that exist in our psychosomatic constitution.

What we are deep down has great importance

What I wanted to emphasize, before we move further ahead – we have a whole year in which to say a lot of things – is this: There's a great importance in what a human being is deep down, every human being, each of us. It's important how we think deep inside, how we move, how we act. And also there's great importance in what I've said in other circumstances and I'll say it again now if you like: What is profoundly the stance we take before the only reality, which is God, and then in the presence of any other reality? Is it the correct position or not?

And so that you understand these things, I'd like to say this. It's not only here in the world where we live and where we don't always have the way and the means necessary to achieve some spiritual success, but even in the desert, in the monasteries – among the hermits, among the ascetics – one sees that there's a very great importance what stance each of them takes before the reality-God and before every other reality.

For example, one sees a man struggling – he prays, he studies, he studies again and again, he tries, he sweats, he keeps vigil. And in the final analysis what happens? He can't achieve any success. This, I repeat, can happen not only here, but even in the hermitages. One discerns that. On the other hand one sees that not merely a simple monk but—let me put it this way – a hermit, a hesychast, who perhaps wears himself out less than another hesychast, he does fewer things than another hermit, and yet God's grace visits him more than the other.

The other hermit keeps vigil and keeps vigil again and again, he fasts, he doesn't eat anything, he takes up disciplines, and yet it appears as if God's grace doesn't take hold of him.

Why? Because the question isn't what one does. I do this, I do that, I do something else and then I add it up. This and that and that and that all together makes up such and such a sum. The question isn't posed like that. The question is what stance the soul takes, man's deeper being, before God, before God's love, God's energies, and before any sort of reality.

Contemporary psychology comes along and tells us this as well.

The basic reason for abnormal psychological conditions

In our previous talk we said that in recent decades great psychologists have appeared who said important things, but that they were also led considerably astray.

And we had emphasized that certain psychiatrists who didn't agree with Freud and Jung – the somewhat newer psychology – maintained that the basic reason, the primary reason, the principle of all the irregular conditions that are present in a human being – from a psychological point of view of course – is the neurotic character structure. But how does one become neurotic?

From a spiritual viewpoint I'd say that this is due to the fact that the deeper being of human existence doesn't take a correct position before the truth, before reality, as I said earlier. As a consequence when the character structure, the innermost recesses of existence, man's deeper being, is neurotic, then neurotic trends or tendencies are created, such as the psychically compulsive drives, anxiety, all those difficulties and all that confusion that, like it or not, contemporary man lives through and can't sort out. And not only does he live an ugly situation, but he doesn't know what's happening to him and he doesn't find any way out.

The deeper reason, then, is the neurotic character structure which is created, as we explained, on account of man's unsound stance before the truth, which is God, and in general before reality. In society reality is what it is. If someone doesn't take a correct position before reality – shall I say if he doesn't have the capability to take a correct position? – if he didn't learn to take a correct position, to be sure he'll get all tangled up. Somewhere his gears will get caught, somewhere he'll get mixed up, and from that point on the man's neurotic symptoms will begin.

And, you see, we're all people who live in the twentieth century and we have the civilization we have and the knowledge we have, but after all no one is a sound human being. Forgive me for saying that. I'd rather not offend anyone, but in any case there's something within us that lures us in one direction or another, sometimes this way, sometimes that. There's something within us that takes us hither and yon. And in this way, as I said, we ourselves are victims of ourselves but we also make others victims.

Blocked in Spite of our Efforts

In Christ Jesus one can be released from any sort of block

As we've said, our effort is to make a deep dive into our existence so that we can see all the parasites, all these foreign elements that create in man the psychological conditions that are not good, and so the person suffers, he endures. Sometimes, to be sure, he reaches the point of getting so entangled in the dark things created inside him that not only can he not disentangle himself, but he loses his head even more. He may want to disentangle himself, he may try, he may even seek help from others, but in the end he doesn't get disentangled and remains mixed up.

The harm that has happened to humanity and particularly to contemporary humanity—that is, to us—is so great that in our effort to disentangle the complications that exist inside us we tangle them up even more. Although sometimes with a puff of air – in the full sense of the term – these things can go away. They can depart from a person once and for all, once and for all they can leave him in peace and in that way the person can be released from those things and see himself, find his God, find his joy and his happiness.

Even though one can, in Christ Jesus, be released from all these entanglements with one breath, in the end it doesn't happen that way. This is the great harm in our days, in our years.

How we managed things… and we adulterated Christianity

If I may be allowed to say so, even Christianity doesn't help us. I'd dare to say that even Christianity is getting tangled up inside us and is itself getting mixed-up. That is, instead of disentangling us, it too becomes a mess inside us. And so one sees people today who believe in God, who study, who want to be considered good Christians, who occupy themselves with others and help them, but in the end there isn't this blue sky in their souls, this clear heaven, this purity and holiness. And their soul isn't simple as it came from the hands of God and as it comes out from the font after baptism; and baptism certainly has power, since the Lord was crucified and resurrected.

This good condition, therefore, is missing. And in spite of the fact that these people who are considered good Christians do this and that and act in this way and the other, the heaven of their souls is clouded and darkened. Not only is there no moon, but there aren't even any stars or any white clouds—just the black clouds that create this whole ugly situation. Certainly not because Christianity is at fault—I said previously that even Christianity fails to help contemporary men – but because – how did we manage it! – we have adulterated even Christianity itself. How did we manage to make even Christianity into a human construction and try in a human way to be released from all the entanglements that exist within us? But that's not how it works.

Let's speak more specifically. Western Christianity started out at the beginning with St. Augustine, but afterwards it was entangled in the scholastic theology of Thomas Aquinas. As great and well-recognized theologians say, it was extended, it was disseminated and cultivated in such a way and reached such a point that instead of freeing man, it enslaves him and blocks him even more. And in the final analysis, while a person is Christian, while he believes in the Gospel, while he believes in Jesus Christ, while he confesses and receives communion, he is blocked. That is – as the great and well-recognized Orthodox theologians, whose research is based on the works of the Church Fathers, say today—we are more influenced by the spirit of western Christianity, which we perhaps call Christian civilization, than by the Christianity of the Gospel and the Fathers, by that Christianity that really redeems a human being, that cleanses man and releases him from all those parasites and from all those pitfalls and makes him pure and clean.

And I think that perhaps we should all do something, one person should do a little and another should do a little, helping one another, so that we can escape the influence of western Christianity, which in the final analysis is a human contraption and not God's Gospel, God's revelation, and God's grace.

Let our soul open to the spirit of the Church Fathers

When one reads the Neptic Fathers who especially occupied themselves with the problems of the human soul and tries to enter their spirit, he sees this comfort, this simplicity that is created in the human soul by God's grace. He feels this breath which obliterates all those things which arise in western Christianity, that human invention. All those snares, all those black and dark things that Christianity of that sort creates in man's soul.

And—what is one to say? – it's a misfortune that while the Gospel is in our hands, while the Fathers—these Neptic, Ascetic, Mystical Fathers, great and lesser, if it is permissible for us to speak in this way—are in our hands, at our disposal, for their works are written in our language; in spite of this our Christian life, what we are trying to live, is influenced only to a very small degree –don't let me say it's not influenced at all – by the Fathers' spirit, by the Fathers' life-altering experiences. It's influenced by a thousand and one other things, by a whole lot of other things, and not by their own spirit. And this is a great misfortune for the Christians of our days.

That's why I said earlier that we should all do something – both we clergy and you laypeople, both those of us who know more and those of us who know less – in order to be helped, so that our self can begin a little at a time to open up a little at a time to that spirit that begins from that point, from the Gospel, from the Fathers, and has reached up to our days and which exists today as well, where it does exist. Let our soul open up so that this breeze can come in, if I may put it in that way, and as soon as it blows, the dark smoke created by mistaken Christianity will go away.

What spiritual life is one to deliver today?

The question, then, isn't just that things are so entangled today and so dark, the question isn't just that for many different reasons contemporary man is so blocked, but also that Christianity, the Christian spirit which prevails today can't release him from his blockage. One would say that it blocks him even more. In fact even Christianity itself is hemmed in there in those blockages in man, as we have said.

And in the final analysis, you see, today we can't say we can see in ourselves this simplicity, this purity, this unblocked condition that God's grace creates, nor can we encounter around us Christians in whom such a condition exists. Instead here we find this and over there we find that – that is, things of a different spirit. And in the final analysis we falsify our Christianity and we falsify ourselves, too.

And to the poor children, to the new generation that comes after us, instead of imparting true spiritual life-altering experiences to them, we deliver to them our blockages, those entangled things. We won't impart words of wisdom to them because words of wisdom accomplish nothing. This is tradition in the Church – one person delivers life to another. But what life is one to give today? He hasn't got any true life to deliver and he delivers those entangled things. And the young people end up taking these things and so Christian life keeps getting worse.

We aren't speaking here and now about people who don't want to believe, who don't want to accept God. Let them do what they want, since that's how they think. We're talking about Christians, about those who believe, about those who want to be and try to be true Christians, but in the final analysis they don't succeed.

We'll keep going, and let's hope something good comes of it in the end.

"That they may be one in Us"

The Trinitarian God and human being-humanity

Man's creator is Trinitarian. This isn't accidental. In our days an effort is taking place, founded on the Church Fathers, to have man enter more deeply into this mystery of the Holy Trinity, into the question of why God is Trinitarian. God is not a monad (a unit) or a dyad – He is a Triad.

The triad symbolizes the infinite, the absolute, while the monad, the dyad and even the tetrad have something circumscribed about them. These questions are an object of study for theologians and each theologian, in accordance with the grace he has from God and his human capabilities, tries to enter more deeply into the mystery. Our God, then, is Trinitarian.

You'll recall that our Lord, in His high priestly prayer,[1] as it is called, that is, the prayer He makes before they capture Him and lead Him to Pilate – as we hear in the first Gospel reading of Holy Thursday evening – beseeches His heavenly Father that His disciples but also others who will believe in Him through the disciples may be one in the Holy Trinity as the Holy Trinity is one. "That they may be one in Us" and "That they may be one as We are one."

Our God is Trinitarian. Man was created in the image and after the likeness of God.[2] And not only is each human being in himself in the image of God, but so is the human-humanity. God made one humanity. So that you understand what I want to say, I am reminding you that the Fathers often

---

[1] See John 17: 1-26.
[2] See Genesis 1: 26. St. Symeon the New Theologian, *On the Mystical Life: The Ethical Discourses*. Vol. 2 *On Virtue and Christian Life*. tr. Alexander Golitzin. Crestwood, NY: St. Vladimir's Seminary Press, 1996, pp. 67-70.

use the singular, man, and they mean all mankind. "God came," they say, "to save man," and they mean all mankind.

Today when we say or hear that "God came to save man," our mind goes to the fact that He came to save this man, that man, that other man. Yes, this is correct. But the phrase "He came to save man" means that He came to save this one humanity. Humanity is one. Man is one as humanity from the viewpoint of his nature in the same way as God is one. The Deity is one, God is one, but three persons. And so humanity is one, one human being, but many persons.

Persons and not individuals

When someone is a monad within God's creation, within this humanity, then he is an individual and he is outside the saved condition which God created, he is outside the true life in Christ. Only when one is a person is he truly within the saved condition, because then he feels that he is the one humanity together with all the other persons-human beings and that he is one human being together with all other persons-human beings.

We aren't inclined to reproach others, but we should say that the individualistic spirit that prevails today came from the West. There for many centuries now there has been cultivated individualism, egocentrism, all that tendency – which exists even today –to speak about man as an individual. This is something degenerate. It's not man's sound condition.

All of us who have found ourselves living today in the twentieth century – whether it is a matter of people who live in the same house, or a matter of people like us now who find ourselves, let's say, in the same auditorium and who are gathered in the name of Christ, or people who live in a large city or in a country or in the whole world – we are this one human being. And in particular it is not simply we who exist today who are the one human being, but also those who came into life up to now and who have left this world, and those who will come in the future, together with us, they are the one human being. This is something that begins with Adam and Eve. In God, in Christ, we are one human being, we are one humanity. Simply put, each of us is a separate person. One is one person, the other is another person, and yet the other is another person.

The persons of the Holy Trinity are three, but they are one God, one Deity, and they have all things in common apart from their properties, apart from the particular characteristics of each person. The Son is the Son. He never becomes the Father. The Father is the Father. He never becomes the Son. The Holy Spirit is the Holy Spirit. He never becomes the Son or the Father.[3] But in the three persons there is one will, one volition, one energy, one love, because the three persons are one Deity.

When, therefore, the Lord asks for people to be united in the three Persons of the Holy Trinity—"that they may be one in Us" – that is, that they be united like the three persons, that's what this means. As in the Holy Trinity all things are in common apart from the characteristic properties of each person, so also human beings must reach such a condition as to be one human being, one humanity, and to have one will, one love, one life – in common – one perfect communion.

George, however, will be George, Costas will be Costas, Basil will be Basil. That is, the particular characteristic of each person is maintained. A person will never lose his

---

[3] See St. John of Damascus, *Exposition of the Orthodox Faith*. Book IV, ch. iv "Why it was the Son of God, and not the Father or the Spirit, that became man: and what having become man He achieved." vol. 9, pp. 75-6 in *Nicene and Post-Nicene Fathers* series. Peabody, MA: Hendrickson Publishers, 1995.

personality, no matter how deep he immerses himself, if I can put it in that way, into the Deity. And before God every human being will be a person, and before other human beings each will have this independence of personality – if I may use this word – while all the other things will be in common.

Where all the problems of the human being are centered

If these things are true, then – and if I have understood correctly that's how things are from the theological, hagiographical, and patristic side – then all the problems of a human being, the problems of a human being as a person, are centered on this problem: How in Christ one will take a sound position before other persons, with Whom he makes up one humanity. That is, each man is not isolated so as to regulate his own affairs independently of others. The whole question is for a man to be able to be situated correctly among other human beings.

If the Christian does not succeed in this in Christ Jesus, then he is completely at sea, mixed up, blocked and he doesn't know what's happening to him. And so he reaches the point of being a Christian and wondering: "Is this how a Christian lives? Are the things the Gospel says right? Is it true what the Fathers say? What's happening to me, after all, that I have this hell inside of me?" Psychologists, as a rule, try to see these questions quite independently of the Gospel and that's why they get mixed up, but we have the light of the Gospel. We have no excuse for getting mixed up.

I gave you an account of a psychologist and psychiatrist, Karen Horney, whose positions have made an impression on me. I think she sees the relevant questions somewhat better than other psychologists – Freud, Adler, Jung – who are considered even today to be great scientists and the fathers of depth psychology. And she sees these things somewhat better precisely because she goes farther than those psychologists.

I think that at this point this psychiatrist begins quite correctly and situates things in an adequately sound manner, certainly from a psychological viewpoint. She kept trying – while she was alive, because she is dead now – with all the work she did and with all the books she wrote, to release people from their blockages. And there is great significance, I think, in the fact that it is this psychiatrist who did not deny, as others did, the ethical and religious consciousness. If we deny these things, she says, we can't do psychology; we can't work on people and help them to really free themselves.[4] She says this, then: The problems begin from one's personality structure, and they are related to the position the person is going to take before other people. A person either moves toward people or against people or away from people.

You see that what happens, happens in relation to other human beings. And this is the basic point in Karen Horney's theory. Other psychologists try to see things somewhat differently, but she places the whole problem in each person and his relationships with other people. That is, she says that a person either moves toward people (certainly in a pathological sense) or moves against people (also in a hostile manner) or moves away from people (that is, he isolates himself, again in a pathological way).

It is noteworthy that in respect to this last point, she immediately observes that there are human beings who live as hermits, complete strangers and far from other human beings, but they do not move away from people in a sick and pathological way. These people find themselves, she says,

4 See *Our Inner Conflicts* pp. 11-12.

to be in a very normal condition, and all human beings are within their hearts. I do not know if she had in mind the great ascetics and hermits of the Orthodox Church, but it impressed me that she immediately makes that observation in order to forestall any misunderstanding.[5]

In the next section we'll try to move forwards with our topic using as a base precisely these three movements of the person.

The bad thing isn't just that we're sinners. God knows that. The bad thing is that we don't go to the Healer, to the Redeemer, Christ.

Whoever truly wants to become a genuine human being must begin with this: "Could it be that I don't see things well? Could it be that I'm not thinking right? Could it be that I'm being led astray? Could it be that I'm not acting correctly? Could it be that I'm a victim of unhealthy conditions, morbid repressed life-experiences that prevail inside me? That are ruling over me and leading me to chaos?"

---

5 See *Our Inner Conflicts* p. 73.

Each of us is a victim of a thousand and one elements and conditions that exist within him. We are led about by various life-altering experiences which act without being under our conscious control. And while we're victims we're unaware of it.

When someone is a monad within God's creation, within humanity, then he is an individual and he is outside the saved condition which God created; he is outside the true life in Christ.

Chapter Two

Moving Toward People

Attachment to Others

A reference to the great psychiatrists

When the great psychiatrists were going to sound man's depths, when they were going to make a dive into the deep part of man's existence, and indeed the existence of contemporary man – the European, the American, but what we are about to say also holds true for the Greeks – so as to help him become unblocked from the blockages that are created within him and to untangle all the entangled things that are deep within him, some of them said one thing and some said another.

One set of things was said by Freud, who made a beginning, laying a basis, a foundation on which he supported his whole theory and all the work he did. And we would say that up until today those who follow Freud's positions also apply his theories and conclusions in their therapy. There is hardly anyone today, however, who follows what Freud said to the letter. In any case, a fair number of people follow him up to a certain point.

Another basis and foundation was laid by Jung, and he built his own theory and all his work on it. And there are also a fair number of those who follow Jung. The third, Adler, had a different basis. These three are the great psychiatrists, and all the others make their beginning from them.

I had told you that a woman psychologist and psychiatrist, who died a few years ago, Karen Horney, who, from what I understood, appeared to have been a good psychologist—naturally she was also a psychoanalyst—was not much in agreement with any of them. With Freud she disagreed quite a bit, but also with Jung. She hardly refers to Adler at all. And in a certain way she sees psychological questions somewhat from her own viewpoint and lays a foundation of her own, a beginning of her own, and builds on it.

I was saying the last time that her positions are better than the corresponding positions of Freud or Jung. She writes that Freud says this on that point, but I don't agree, and I think something else is correct. Jung says this on that point, but I don't agree, and I think something else is correct.

Personally, from what I know, I believe her positions are closer to the truth. Of the positions of the others, some are not convincing and others are completely unacceptable. But even certain other positions that might have been acceptable at first aren't convincing in the final analysis. On the contrary, her positions are quite convincing.

Among other things – as I said previously – she is particularly at odds with Freud about the fact that he gave no importance to ethics, that is, to the ethical consciousness, we would say. We're doing science, he said. What business do those things have with science? How is it possible, says Karen Horney, for anyone to do psychology, psychotherapy, psychoanalysis, that is, to occupy oneself with human beings, in whom this ethical consciousness exists—whether you want it or not, it exists – and not to take it into account? When you ignore it – this psychiatrist emphasizes – something will be missing from the whole structure you're building, something will be left out of the foundation you're laying.[1] Since this exists, however, in the end it will cause your structure to explode in the air and will make you out a liar.

This psychiatrist, then, considers that all a person's blockages – "blockage" is a beautiful word, and I think it does a good job of conveying this phenomenon we notice in contemporary man – all these blockages are due or have

---

[1] See *Our Inner Conflicts* pp. 24-7.

some relationship with one of the three movements a person can make in relation to other people.

One is moving toward people.

The second is moving against people.

And the third is moving away from people.

These theses of Karen Horney's – remember, we were talking about them – appear to be an adequately good foundation psychologically, theologically, and spiritually.

With true love we take a correct position before others

We have said that God made one humanity. And as the Deity is one from the viewpoint of nature, but three persons, so the human being is one as mankind but many persons. God made man in His image. Certainly when we say that man came to be in the image of God, we mean this, that, and the other thing, but in the phrase "in the image of God" there is also the meaning that man is not a monad, that man as humanity is many persons. Basically this means that man cannot stand, he cannot exist, as a monad. Somehow within the root of his existence there are also others.

This, in the final analysis, means that we cannot ignore the existence of others. It means that we cannot ignore it with our mind, but also that we cannot ignore it with our life, with our existence. It means further that if this or that man doesn't take a correct position before the other men together with whom he comes from one root – they are one root, one man, one humanity all together – somehow he won't be able to develop correctly, normally. And beyond the fact that he'll be lost, he'll perish from the theological and spiritual viewpoint, furthermore he'll be blocked. That is, that all these blockages of a psychological nature will be created inside him and he'll stay completely confused.

So man needs to take the correct position before others. And we would say that theologically, biblically, evangelistically, one is situated correctly before others with love. With the love of God, though, with the love that is not bound, is not given as a favor, has no second thoughts, and does not "seek its own."[2]

With love a person takes the correct position before other people. Among the Persons of the Holy Trinity there exists a communion of love. And among men there must exist this communion of love, of true love.

I am saying this and emphasizing it, that there must exist the communion of true love, because we often think we love or that we go to a lot of trouble for love and we make a big deal of it, and it's possible that deep down we don't have true love. A mother, for example, can go to great lengths, can fall to pieces for her children, and in the final analysis the position she takes before her children may not be the correct position, may not be a position of love, but something else.

So when a person doesn't take the correct position before other men, that is, when he has no love, true love, within him and then he will take before others one of those three positions which we mentioned and which Karen Horney discusses. And I think – it's possible I'm in error – that in some way, her position can also stand up spiritually and theologically.

The need for someone to be attached somewhere

The first position is moving toward people. This means attachment to other people. For example, the mother can be attached to the child. The wife can be attached to her husband or the husband to his wife. The spiritual child can be

---

2 1 Corinthians 13: 4-5.

attached to his spiritual father. And how can one then resolve the question why this spiritual child makes no progress in the spiritual life? – this spiritual child who – if I may be permitted to mention a few things in hyperbole—night and day can confess and be considered the most dedicated child, the most dedicated Christian. In the final analysis, however, since he did not take the correct position before his spiritual father, but attached himself to him, he has no true progress. It's impossible for him to have any. How is he going to have true progress? Man cannot be true when separated from his foundation, when separated from his basis.

Moving toward people, then, is this attachment. The mother is attached to her child, the parents to their children or the children to their parents. How many children, girls but also boys – to include the stronger sex grow up and can't detach themselves from their mother. They get married and still this attachment exists.

Or how many people are there who can't live without depending on something? That is, one clings—and let's not talk about things—onto people, one becomes dependent on people and one can't live without this dependency. This isn't a true position. A man of this sort can't have a true faith in his soul, nor can he say, "I believe in God, I have God within me. Christ came into the world for me, too."

We would say that this movement toward other people, this attachment starts out from selfishness—if we look at the question from the spiritual viewpoint, disregarding what this psychiatrist is saying—it starts out from a self-complacency, from fears, from a feeling of insecurity. That is, this person who is attached can't stand on his own two feet, and that's why he must grab onto something.

Don't say, though, that what Paul the Simple, a novice monk, has done is attachment. As we read in the

Synaxaristes,[3] he came to Antony the Great with the aim of becoming a monk as a disciple at his side. When Antony the Great opened the door and saw him, he asked him what he wanted. "I came," he replied, "to become a disciple." Antony the Great presented his objections, but St. Paul insisted. Finally St. Antony went into his cell and left him outside to wait. And after three days he came out of his cell again. That man was waiting outside in the blistering heat without food.

What St. Paul did, since he came to learn, isn't a manifestation of attachment, it isn't a manifestation of this sick condition that exists in us. No. It's an expression of great courage, of great faith and great love for God.

One can go to the greatest teacher to learn and become a well-rounded scholar without being attached. Or one can go to an elder and learn without being attached. This attachment we're discussing is something of a sickness.

One must not even be attached to God

Should I dare to say that one must not even be attached to God? Perhaps this appears strange, but it can happen. And I need to explain. We often have recourse to God and call upon Him and ask for what we want and we don't receive any hint of an answer. Why? Because we go with such a spirit of attachment. Of course God doesn't accept anything of the sort. Because for one to be attached, if I may be allowed to say this – it can be that I'm in error, now these thoughts are coming into my mind – it's like suicide. How could God allow a man to kill himself? One who becomes attached puts himself to death ethically and spiritually. Attachment is a spiritual suicide. God can't accept this.

---

3 See *The Great Synaxaristes of the Orthodox Church*. March. Buena Vista, CO: Holy Apostles Convent, Dormition Skete, 2005. pp. 140-7.

We must approach God with humility. And here's where things get tangled up. The other fellow has a spirit of attachment and he attaches himself and thinks he's humble. And when someone shows him that he needs to humble himself, he's bewildered. "Who, me? Humble myself? I who am dust and ashes?" But his feelings belong to the spirit of attachment and not to the spirit of humility. So the one who has recourse to God humbles himself and becomes dust and ashes, but he doesn't kill himself.

The one who attaches himself will call on God again and again and if he doesn't get an answer he'll lose hope and be disappointed. While the one who truly humbles himself and is contrite before God – the more God doesn't answer him, the more he hopes. It seems strange, and yet that's how it is. The longer God takes to answer, the longer God takes to intervene, the more he hopes. He is not discouraged, but keeps on hoping.

The true novice isn't attached to his elder. He humbles himself and learns virtue. So one must not attach oneself to anyone – not even to God.

If this unhealthy situation, in one way or the other, in this way or otherwise, rules over a man, and, unknowingly, he fosters it, maintains it, and maybe even sees it as virtue and brags about it, it's something frightful. It's not simply a bad thing, but something frightful. And if one isn't rescued from it, he'll be outside the true path, outside the true foundation on which the true human being is built.

But let's not wear you out anymore today. We'll proceed in somewhat the same way with respect to the other two movements of a person, and we'll have all the time we need to say ample things about them.

Unhealthy Compliance

In this series of talks we're trying to get to know ourselves better both psychologically and spiritually.

We've said that man doesn't come into this world alone – not just in the sense that others also exist around him, but also in the sense that in his existence things are such that he's bound together with others.

Man doesn't exist by himself, but rather he exists together with others. As a consequence it's very important – as we've explained in previous gatherings – what position one takes before others. Whether he wants to or not, he'll take a position before others. Even for him to avoid others and isolate himself and declare war against them is a position before them. If, then, the position one will take before others isn't the correct one but is wrong, all his torments will begin from that point on.

We've also said that in order for one to take a correct position before other people, of course one must take a correct position before God. Similarly when one does take a correct position before other people, one also takes a correct position before God.

And remember that we've emphasized that when no real love exists in a person, the position he's going to take before other human beings – just as whether he wants to or not, he will take some position—will be incorrect. And this incorrect movement of his before other people is manifested in three ways. There can be many others, but perhaps they are all contained in these three ways. One way is manifested in one person, a second in another, and the third way in a third person. Or two of the three can be manifested in one person and all three together in another.

We've been saying that a person who doesn't have a true, genuine love within him either attaches himself to other people or takes a hostile position before them or else he's indifferent about other people and isolates himself. And we've said that we'll try to examine these three movements of a person before others somewhat better.

Compulsive pursuit of the other

Let's take the first case, moving toward other human beings. When a person attaches himself to other people, when he complies with them, what happens? At first everyone who truly loves other human beings can appear to have an attachment, but that's not the way it is. His love is something pure, something genuine, something true.

When one doesn't have true love, however, when basically one is unhealthy psychologically and spiritually, then the pursuit of the other has a sick character. In this case the attachment to the other and compliance with him is something that creates an ever-uglier situation in the one who has the attachment. This situation neither lets him live spiritually nor does it allow him from the psychological viewpoint to have the balance and inner freedom he needs to live easily and freely as a free personality. The first characteristic in this person is the pursuit of love and approval of the other. He feels this as a need. And as psychology says, this need is a compulsive situation.

To make myself clearer let me say this. Everyone seeks the love of others, everyone more or less seeks the approval and companionship of others. But he who feels this need in an unhealthy way and has this pursuit and this tendency inside him, when he sees that people don't love him, when he sees that they don't approve of him, when he doesn't find the companionship he seeks, he's immediately overtaken by anguish and by an ugly psychological situation which doesn't allow him to be at peace and to feel free as a human being. It doesn't let him stand on his own two feet and feel some balance psychologically. But it also doesn't allow him to make progress spiritually, as we've said.

Please don't hesitate at all to believe that there are more people than we think who have this tendency, who are dominated by these compulsive situations.

Personally, from what I know, from what I understand, from what I observe and monitor, I'd say that a great number of today's Christians are more or less affected by this rather deep morbid situation, and that's why these Christians don't make spiritual progress, they cannot make spiritual progress. So let me say that their Christian life seems counterfeit. Sometimes they themselves understand it, and sometimes they don't. Sometimes they choose to recognize it and to admit it, and sometimes they choose not to. But others understand that their life is a counterfeit, a false, a hypocritical Christian life – not in the sense of raw hypocrisy, but unconsciously.

From this point on, we understand how much the Christian presence is deteriorating in our days, how much this witness is deteriorating which as Christians we are called to give in the world.

When this witness of ours, this presence of ours, our whole Christian life, both from the psychological and from the spiritual side, is counterfeit, is not genuine, we can understand – when we don't understand, it's even worse – how much harm we do both in general in the world and in the society in which we live, but also to the body of the Church and to us ourselves.

A consequence of unhealthy compliance toward others

And so these human beings who feel the necessity of attachment and have the tendency of compliance – the word "compliance" is a psychological term – seek to rely on something. And such a person, such a Christian can – why should we be ashamed to say it? – be attached to someone, because this person gave him what he has been seeking. That is, the other person satisfied his need for love, for approval, for companionship. The reason he attaches himself is that this person seeks these things not as a free personality, not as a human being who is moved by genuine love and by a genuine disposition to come into relationship with others, but moved by a sick condition, by a sick disposition and tendency. Such a Christian, then, relies on another person or persons who, as we have said, at first satisfied his sick disposition in some way, he hooks himself onto them, and he can be bound together with them in such a way that from that point on he sees nothing else and he can't separate himself from the other person or the other people to whom he is attached. He sees in them only those virtues, let's say, only those good points which exactly satisfy his own sick condition. And you understand what happens from this point on.

For that reason sometimes we see a person follow another blindly, and we may wonder: "What does he find in that person to follow him and comply with him so faithfully, almost blindly? How is it that he doesn't see in him whom he follows, toward whom he is compliant, on whom he depends, and with whom he's bound, certain great and striking shortcomings?" And yet he doesn't see them.

This person who has a compulsive inner tendency and impulse such as we said is in a position to be blinded and not to see even in himself anything good that he has and that the other doesn't have, but also not to see in the other to whom he is attached anything bad that perhaps exists and which makes him not to be a true or genuine guide. And so he makes him his guide and from now on this is the person he relies on, depends on, with whom he is bound and with whom he complies to the letter and in all details.

I repeat, this happens because this man cannot stand on his own two feet and feel free in himself. He cannot see other human beings with love as a separate personality, be moved toward them with true love and come into a true relationship with them.

The morbid pursuit of love

This man seeks to be liked in a compulsive way, in a morbid and sick way. He seeks love, approval, support, protection. And he seeks them to such a point that, if they are lacking – if I may say this – not only does he feel uneasy, not only can he not find any peace, not only can he not calm down, but he feels as if he's lost, he feels as if he's sinking into chaos.

Perhaps sometimes he tries to break away, but the moment he goes to break away he sees that something is slipping away under his feet and he's sinking into chaos and going to be destroyed. And so as not to be destroyed he gives himself with a greater impulse to that sick thing, to that relationship and condition that is not genuine, not natural, and not normal.

Allow me to say that the only thing that preoccupies such a person is not to lose the fact that others like him, the fact that they love him, not to lose that protection, that approval. That preoccupies him. From that point on, he's ready to do the most difficult, the most humiliating jobs. He's ready to do things that someone else would be amazed to see him doing. Of course, all these things occur so that something unhealthy can be preserved, so that something unhealthy can be increased, something that is psychologically and spiritually not healthy – consequently, to preserve something which is in no way pleasing before God.

Here we need to note the following: As much as such a person feels subconsciously and deeply within himself that he needs love – this unhealthy love – that he needs this approval of others, to the same degree he also thinks that other human beings are in need and runs to them as a helper, but certainly in an unhealthy way. I'm sorry, but that's the way it is. Don't be at all surprised if I tell you that this person is the most eager to run from one human being to another who is in need, all day and sometimes at night – certainly not out of real love. Don't let that seem at all strange to you. And the proof is that while these tasks are tasks that have the fragrance of sanctity, while they are "labors" of a saint, while these manifestations are manifestations of a saint, this person who avails himself of the whole day and the whole night to do work of that sort, does not have the fragrance of sanctity. Something basic is lacking to him.

This person moves in this way –I brought a simple example – purely and simply in order not to miss hearing "good job" from someone. Possibly this "good job" isn't spoken in words, but the other person can, for example, show with his whole attitude that he is satisfied, pleased, he can show that he approves of the other person, that he loves him, that he defends him.

It's possible for these people to reach a point where it appears to others that they are acting unselfishly, altruistically, that they're acting in such a way that they're sacrificing themselves for the good of others. But in a basic sense, they are doing nothing but serving the tendency they have, that is, not to lose this love they expect from somewhere. Wherever they found it, they grabbed it and from that point on they're really ready to come apart, really to destroy themselves, as long as they can prevent the loss of that unhealthy life-experience, that unhealthy satisfaction.

What we're saying is the truth

We've cited these things as examples. A person who suffers from such a compulsive tendency can have many different symptoms.

I believe what we're saying at this moment is all true. I believe it not only because psychology helps us in some way to understand them, but also because personally, from the little experience I have, I ascertain that this is how things are. You see, as we've said, a person in a sweat from running continually here and there to help, and on the other hand you can't discern a drop of grace within his soul, you can't discern even the slightest presence of God within him. He's in a sweat as he runs here and there, but one senses that all this hard work he's doing, all this effort, is happening in order for this unhealthy condition to be preserved – that is, so he doesn't lose the love and companionship he's seeking.

Well, I believe this is how things are, not only because contemporary psychology presents it somewhat in this way, not only because I, too, personally, from the small experience I have, ascertain that this is how things are, but also because one draws such a conclusion very easily, without great difficulty, from the Church Fathers and especially from the most austere Fathers, from those called the Neptic Fathers. One often sees, apart from other things – let's just give one example – elders, spiritual fathers, experienced ascetics, enlightened psychologically – psychology would say – completely balanced human beings, well, one sees that these great ascetics sometimes attribute absolutely no importance at all to such activities and expressions of their spiritual children. And at first sight one thinks they're acting harshly. At first sight one thinks that it's as if their position, what they are doing, isn't very humane. And yet deeply their position isn't harsh at all and their behavior isn't harsh at all.

In reality, they're struggling to protect their spiritual children from sick and pathological conditions, from all those conditions which aren't at all spiritual and have no relation with genuine Christian life-experience, with true Christianity.

Let us not hesitate

If, then, what we're saying at this moment is true, on the one hand you understand why we aren't making any progress, despite our putting in a certain effort, and on the other hand one understands how much hard work gets lost. If it were simply that the hard work is getting wasted, this is nothing. But the question is that there is no expectation, there is no hope for one to find the correct road, if one continues in this way and cannot disengage, cannot free himself. He'll be led astray and in the end he won't accomplish anything in spite of his struggle and his efforts.

If, then, what we're saying is how things are – and I repeat, I believe that it is, and I gave you my reasons – then we must not hesitate, we must not fear, we must not slack off, no matter how much trouble we encounter, to cast a glance, each of us, at himself, in case something deeper within us isn't going right. That is, just in case, in the final analysis, each of us, with whatever we do and don't do, "is seeking himself," as the Fathers say. And we'll find ourselves, but "to our own perdition." Because, when one seeks the love of others in a sick way, then he seeks to satisfy his selfishness, as the Fathers say. That is, it could be that in the final analysis we are doing this and that, but in all of these things "we are seeking our own" and we keep finding ourselves, but to our own destruction and also for the harm of others.

When, however, we make this inquiry, we make this dive into ourselves and somewhere we grab hold of something and first we understand it, we recognize it and subsequently we do what is necessary, God is capable of redeeming man from whatever he has wrong with him and leading him to the true road, leading him to true love, to salvation.

Submission Which Doesn't Liberate

As you know, with these talks we're making an effort to go deeper into the human psyche, to be able in this way to know ourselves better and consequently to take a truer position before God. And so that when we take a suitable position, God can favor us and bless us.

We dedicated the short time of our talk last time to the morbid movement toward other people which appears in certain people whether they understand it or not. And we were saying that the very first characteristic of those people who have been attacked by this illness is that they are compliant toward what others say, seek, and require.

And more particularly, we were saying that these people do everything, they even lower their dignity in order to be able to ensure the love and the esteem of others, in order to be able in some way to have the applause and approval of others. Remember, we spoke at some length about this matter.

It's possible that when many Christians run here and there to help, they think they're doing a good deed and that they're among the best Christians. And certainly, taken by itself, this effort may be good, but the question is why they're doing what they're doing.

If, then, each person asks and searches himself, he'll see that most often he does many such things solely in order to be able to secure the love, esteem, and approval of others and especially of some person to whom he has attached himself. And this certainly can't be Christianity, no matter how Christian these expressions appear.

Healthy and unhealthy submission

Another characteristic of these people is submission.

Certainly submission or obedience is a virtue in the Church. And as you know, monastics have an obligation to carry out obedience. When they're tonsured, along with two other vows they also make the vow that they'll be obedient, that they'll be submissive to the abbot, to the elder, to the spiritual father. With obedience they'll cut off their will. With this submission they'll be able to be redeemed, with God's grace and assistance, from the old man, from their passions and their desires, and they'll move forward to their rebirth.

But you see there's also unhealthy submission, which doesn't liberate a person, submission which doesn't help a person to become free from passions, selfishness, from his own will, from the old man, and to arrive at true and real rebirth.

This submission is an illness which renders people who are attacked by it unable to see clearly what they themselves are and what others are. That is, it causes them to overestimate others and see false virtues and false talents in them. We must certainly say once again that there's no harm in seeing others as higher and oneself as lower. On the contrary it's a good thing when it's healthy. When it's an unhealthy thing, however, it does a great deal of harm. The reason one arrives at such an unhealthy submission is that he doesn't dare to see with his eyes open, very clearly, what that human being is to whom he's submitting himself, what that human being is to whom he has attached himself and to whom he has bound himself.

He doesn't dare because if he allows himself to see with his eyes wide open and consequently lowers the level of his submission somewhat – this attachment of his – afterwards he can't bear it, he can't stand on his own two feet, he can't cope with life. And this happens because he's someone who, only if he grabs hold somewhere, only if he leans on something, only if he sees even some false virtues somewhere, false gifts, can he stand on his own feet. Only then can he live, can he can feel somewhat calm, somewhat comfortable, and not be overwhelmed by an inner chaos, by an inner turmoil and uneasiness which leads him to destruction. The bad thing is that he himself sees it as a virtue. But also that person or those persons to whom he is attached, to whom he submits himself slavishly, on whom he depends in a servile way, they consider it, as we were saying last time, as a virtue.

As you can see, if this is true – and for me it's completely true – then we have an utter falsification of Christian life, an utter falsification and adulteration of Christian life-altering experiences. And there comes about a humliation to this person, who nourishes a hope that something is happening with him, that is, that in the end he will benefit. But instead of seeing a benefit, instead of being helped, he's destroyed. But the other person, too, who accepts this unhealthy submission and cultivates it, harms both himself and the one who subordinates himself to him.

Slavish dependence on others

Another characteristic of these sick people is dependence. People who have this illness can't live without dependence on others. Their self-esteem depends on the approval or disapproval others show them, on the opinion others have about them.

How many people, good Christians in other respects, are burdened in the literal sense of the term – they can't sleep at night or they can't calm down the following day, they can't do their chores and say their prayers. That is, they literally lose themselves and are dominated by an inner chaos – because this, that, or the other person on whom they are dependent – perhaps in an unconscious manner, perhaps without realizing it – didn't speak nicely to them, didn't show them the approval they were anticipating, didn't say "well done" to them, or "good job" as they were expecting.

If you wish, let's speak more specifically. If, for example, we're waiting for someone to visit us – and we desire this visit a great deal – and in the end he doesn't do it, we may not say anything to anyone, we may hide what we felt when he didn't come, but basically the whole good idea we had about ourselves will drop to the lowest point – it will be reduced to nothing.

While this person was smiling at us, while he was saying the sort of words that allowed us to understand that we were in his favor, while he was conducting himself toward us in such a way that it appeared he was our friend, that he esteemed us, that he took account of us, we felt good, at ease, we felt that we ourselves were something in society. But as soon as he turned his back, as soon as with a certain word of his, with his whole position, for example, with his refusal or his failure to visit us – who knows what his reasons were for not doing it – he showed that he didn't esteem us anymore, everything inside us was destroyed.

These people, that is, the sick types who are suffering from something of the sort, they can't calm down afterwards, they can't find peace, they can't find rest. And they're ready, eager to do whatever happens to be necessary – whatever they think will appease the other, will cause him to esteem them again, to approve of them again – what they think will help them to secure his love again. They're ready to conduct themselves slavishly and to lose their dignity and become ridiculous.

From what I understand – I may be wrong –there are Christians today, faithful, more than we think exist, who live with such an inner disorder, with such an inner chaos. And it's absolutely impossible –let me put it this way – for such a Christian to progress in the spiritual life.

To such a soul, which, whether it understands it or not, whether it wants or not, is attached to others and depends on others in such a manner that, one would say, it awaits the love of others as if God Himself, it isn't possible for God's grace to come and take up residence, for God's blessing to come, for Christ to come. It isn't possible for Christ to live in such a soul—according to the verse, "It is no longer I who live, but Christ lives in me."[1] Because this soul has lost itself, it has slipped away from itself and relies on something else. A certain person has captured the soul. The soul has been possessed by all these things, which are idols.

Repressed hostility and strange outbursts

But the harm goes further. A human being who is moved in such a way toward others, who is attached to others and bound with them and depends on them in such a manner that in some way he looks them in the eyes to see whether they'll laugh or not, whether they'll approve of him or not, whether they'll esteem him or not, such a human being doesn't suffer from that alone. He also suffers from the other things we have mentioned.

That is, he may also have within him tendencies of hostility toward others. Certainly the more he senses that he's a slave of others and that others are exploiting him, in

---

[1] Galatians 2:20.

some way the more the tendency of hostility towards them flares up. But if he manifests his hostility, if he manifests his aggressive dispositions toward others, he immediately loses their love, their approval – precisely what he's waiting for from them in order to support himself and ensure in this way his peace and tranquility. So because he fears losing this love, this favor of others, that's why he sometimes suppresses this protest that comes from within him, about which one should say let it be expressed once and for all.

He suppresses this protest which begins from within him, he suppresses the impulse he feels to protest, to react, or to attack. Not that these are good things, but we're talking now about what's happening inside this person's soul. So he suppresses these things – as psychology would say, he represses them – and even he himself doesn't want to know that he has them, let alone for others to know!

These things, however, do exist within these people. As they are repressed, they exist in the soul and somehow or other, at one time or another, they'll burst forth from inside there to bite whoever they can.

That's why we see in such people who attach themselves, who are extremely disciplined, who are extremely obedient, extremely good – and one can ask them to do something and they do it easily, or one can send them here and there and they go, or set them to sweating and straining all day long doing this and that and they do it – well, we see in these people that there comes a moment when this repressed reality of reaction, of protest, of disposition toward aggression, can no longer remain hidden, and these people explode. And that's why it's not rare to see these people – who appear on the one hand so good – react in such a way that makes others wonder.

This also happens sometimes with children. Many children are slavishly attached to their parents. And this happens because their personality is very defective, and they can't bear to cope by themselves. And so they grab on, they hang onto their mother, their father. They appear to be very sensible and very obedient children, they appear to be the best children – so we think – while deep down they're sick. And that's why sometimes such a child becomes unrecognizable, and one says: This child who was so good – how did he turn out like this? How is it that he expresses himself in this way? Adults can also manifest the same thing. A moment can come that they'll manifest themselves and react in such a way, they'll protest and attack in such a way that one would wonder. And sometimes this attack, this protest, this whole reaction is expressed, I would say, passively. It's that grievance, that bitterness, that disappointment, that hopelessness, that is observed in these human beings.

Double trouble

If these things are true, and if these things are, more or less, in the hearts of today's Christians, then woe to us if we don't become conscious of them, if we don't understand them and don't recognize exactly what's happening to each of us. And woe to us if we can't – either by ourselves or with the assistance of someone else or some other persons – escape from this situation and we remain in it. It's not just that we won't make progress in the spiritual life. So many today want to make progress in the spiritual life and they don't make progress. But that's not the only trouble. The trouble is that all the Christianity we have within us, all of this Christendom we express in this way or that and that we present to the contemporary world is illegitimate.

Contemporary man – even those roisterers and whoever else – basically wants salvation. And the hour comes that he seeks salvation. As he comes into communion with us contemporary Christians, however – who don't have within us genuine Christianity, genuine Christian life-changing experiences, but an illegitimate situation and unhealthy, illegitimate things, tangled-up Christian life-experiences, in accordance with what we've said – today's man, then, senses that something isn't going right here, and he can't hope that if he becomes Christian, if he believes in God, he'll find something better, he'll be saved. He senses that not only will he not find anything better, but maybe he'll get tangled up even worse, and that's why he draws back. Or, if someone turns up who is going to follow us, he himself will fit into our own mold and in the end he'll become like us.

I've said it often enough here and elsewhere. It seems to me that Christianity has lost much of its authenticity today. Certainly all of life has become disingenuous today. Wherever you go, life is disingenuous in all its manifestations and in all its expressions. But Christianity has become disingenuous, too. Christianity in itself is authentic, but the way we're living it, the way we express it and present it is impure, illegitimate, fake.

As a consequence the trouble is twofold. We do harm both to ourselves and to others. God will certainly be gracious. We don't know what He will do to us when we leave this world, but as long as we're here and we live like this, we aren't going to progress spiritually. That is, we aren't going to see a miracle really take place within us. But we're also doing great harm to others because we're not a genuine witness of Christianity. We're not a true witness of the Gospel, of God's revelation to the world, and consequently we can't help the world while we have an obligation to do so.

Love as an Unwholesome Expression

We've been speaking about people who appear to be good Christians but who are attacked in some way by a certain psychic illness, by a certain spiritual illness, and more particularly by that illness which causes them to seek the approval and esteem of others and to have their peace of mind dependent on others, on what position others take before them.

It's worthwhile today for us to say a couple of words more about the question of love as it presents itself to such people.

What is the person seeking who places a great importance on love in an unhealthy way?

These unhealthy types—and let me say once again that there are not a few people who are attacked by this illness – these unhealthy types place a great importance on love. And in particular not only do they themselves think they are occupying themselves with something very holy, very sacred, very important, but so do others around them as they see them and follow them, admire them. In reality, though, this love which has become an obsession in them is something morbid, something unhealthy. Certainly love, taken by itself, is what remains forever, but the love these types have and express is a morbid life-experience, a morbid expression and a morbid activity.

As we've said, these morbid types are those people who seek the love, the affection, the approval of others and depend greatly on the favor and good position of others before them. And they do this because otherwise they can't stand on their own two feet, or, better, they aren't even capable of living.

That's why in the end they reach a point where they talk about love all the time, where they seek love all the time, where they praise love all the time, with the result, as I said, that they themselves think that they've found the right path and others think this person or those people have really found the right path. Let alone now that these people themselves who always seek and search for and imagine love and talk about love all the time have no happiness within them, have no joy or peace within them, but they live continually with an anguish, with an emptiness that never fills, they live continually with a pursuit which is never fulfilled.

This tendency, then, is an unhealthy situation. Something of this sort serves a neurotic type —as psychologists call him – very well. That is, for him to speak in such a way about love, to seek love in such a way and to elevate this type of love up to heaven. It serves him very well. That is, it serves the compulsive and contradictory and unhealthy tendencies he has within him. Love serves such a type of person because in this way he will be liked by others – something he seeks a great deal, that he aims at a great deal – and because at the same time he'll feel that he has control over them.

Whoever has the guts to do it – if you want me to put it like this—let him observe himself or the people closest to him. He'll see that many of them who walk up and down the stairs of homes, who go in and out of houses of needy people, who run around with the word "love" in their mouth, who are ready to perish for this love, many of them literally beat themselves and melt for love with the following two considerations as ulterior motives: on the one hand to be liked by others, to ensure their favor in this way and to lean on something, to support themselves, to be able to stand on their feet, and on the other hand to admire themselves for the control they have over others. Because such a person who helps another who has a need – who comes, for example, as a helper to a handicapped person – feels that the other person is a lesser human being, and he's of a superior sort, who can do this and that.

He's served a great deal by love, then, because he succeeds in being liked, a thing that his very self seeks a great deal and needs, and with love he also succeeds in having control over others. He feels a great need to have control, he seeks it a great deal, and he can't bear to be below others.

Certainly we said last time that such a type subordinates himself, he's dependent, he's literally broken in pieces before others, but in the final analysis he does all these things in order not to lose the love and affection of others. On the other hand, however, he must find a person or people that he himself feels superior to, that he dominates and has control over in the sense that he can offer them this or that service in order to hear "thank you" so that they'll be humbled in this way before him. At the same time, such a type is the person who, with the way he expresses love, that he thinks about love, that he seeks it here and there, shows that he feels a need to be in second place. Never can such a person be in first place, for example, be a guide, be a leader, never can he completely take up the responsibility for certain actions, expressions, and activities. He feels the need to be in second place and for someone else to be above, who takes up the responsibilities.

On the one hand, then, he wants to be in second place, but on the other hand he wants to be in first place. That is, with love – such as we have spoken about – he manages things in a certain way so that the others whom he serves, whom he thinks about, the others from whom he seeks love and to whom he gives love, for them to be above him and consequently for him to be in second place. At the same time, however, he himself feels that he is above. That is, that he himself is the one who has understood life – in his own opinion certainly – he has found the right path, he has grasped the meaning of love and, having this and giving that, he accomplishes everything. And so he gloats over himself.

Love and hostility—a strange combination

As we were saying last time, however, while on the one hand these people look everywhere for the love, the affection, the favor of others, on the other hand they have within them aggressive and hostile dispositions toward others. They have an impulse within them to tear the other apart if possible. But they repress these aggressive, hostile dispositions, they bury them inside themselves and not even they themselves want to know that they exist. Because if such an aggressive, hostile element comes out into the open, then the affection from others is gone, and there goes all the love and approval they're expecting from others. It's precisely for this reason that they bury all these things inside them.

But these things exist, in keeping with what we've said on other occasions. No matter how much one represses something within himself, it exists and acts from there. Consequently these aggressive tendencies and dispositions exist there inside this person and they are going to emerge. They, too, seek their rights. So when these people speak about love, when they elevate it high and when they have love as an ideal – unhealthy love, of course – these aggressive dispositions that they have are to some extent taken care of. As we said earlier, these people, even if not out in the open, but certainly secretly inside condemn all the other people, they accuse them and believe that all human beings act incorrectly, that they have not found their way.

As these people believe that the highest ideal, the sum of everything is love – they really do believe it, they really do accept it in that way—basing themselves on this, completely unencumbered, with a great deal of ease, without understanding it, they condemn others and accuse those who have not found what they themselves have found, who haven't understood what they have understood, who don't work at this high ideal where they work. They also manage in this way, then, to satisfy these aggressive tendencies they have within themselves. That is, in some way it's as if they're giving nourishment to them when they speak about love, when they position love as an ideal in their lives, this love that's like a phantom in front of them. Wherever they find themselves, wherever they stand, when they go to bed and when they get up, this is what holds them together. That is, they've suffered from a sort of psychosis on the subject of love – unhealthy love, I repeat, and not healthy love.

But this, however, isn't therapy. This isn't adjustment. And that's the reason for the continued existence of the consequences created by these inner conflicts, these repressions, this unhealthy situation in general. And in the final analysis the person doesn't find the peace he seeks, though he has "love" in front of him as a phantom, and though, from a certain angle, he thinks he's the only person who has found the truth, the only one who's working correctly. And so, whether he wants to or not, whether he understands or not, he lives out this drama, he lives out this emptiness. He lives out this ugly situation created by the inner conflicts.

Here let me add the following. A great many souls, miserable souls, and both on the part of boys and on the part of girls – perhaps more on the part of girls, but also on the part of the boys I know – a great many souls, as they are possessed by this pursuit of love, they seek this morbid, false, unhealthy love in the fleeting relationships they create.

How many miserable souls spend today like this, tomorrow like that, today with this companion, tomorrow with that. And they do this because, as I've said, they consider this unhealthy and morbid love to be an ideal thing, and so they seek to fill the emptiness they feel, they seek to fill their souls, to find peace, tranquility. Impossible. It's utterly impossible. Certainly others seek, cultivate, and express this love in other directions.

Could it be that I am a victim of unhealthy conditions?

The great trouble that exists in these human beings – and we've said that quite a few are affected by this illness – the great trouble isn't that they find themselves in this situation, but that they don't understand it. It's almost impossible to understand it unless one begins with "could it be?" – "Could it be that I'm mistaken? Could it be that I didn't understand well? Could it be that I'm not acting correctly?" – and in this way to find someone who can help. Otherwise, it's almost impossible for these people to suspect that this love they seek and which they have elevated so high, which they've made into a phantom and an ideal, this love isn't genuine love, it isn't true love, but an unhealthy condition, and they themselves are victims of it. They can't understand this so as to try to see things from another point of view.

In addition, in their intoxication with love – if you want me to put it this way – which is created in their thinking and in their emotional world they can't suspect that within them there's also a lot of hatred, a lot of enmity. Nested within them there's also a lot of aggression flaring up, a lot of savagery and a lot of malice. They can't suspect this. Don't let anyone dare to tell them anything of the sort. It's like striking a snake on the tail. You know that if someone strikes a snake on the tail, the snake bites him. The snake is overpowered only if one strikes it on the head. If you strike it on the tail, it bites you afterward. Well, when someone dares in this way to bring to light a few such things that exist in the depth of their soul, it's like striking the snake on the tail. They'll be surprised, they'll dash at you, of course without realizing it themselves they'll react in such a way as to silence you and make you change your own mind. And so the trouble persists.

That's why we say again and again that whoever happens to want to have the genuine life created truly within him, whoever truly wants to become a genuine human being, a man of God, must begin with this: "Could it be that I don't see things well? Could it be that I'm not thinking right? Could it be that I'm led astray? Could it be that I'm not acting correctly? Could it be that I'm a victim of unhealthy conditions, repressed morbid life-experiences, and all these things take me here and there, they prevail within me, they rule over me, and in the final analysis instead of becoming a genuine human being, instead of becoming a child of God, I'm becoming a victim of all those things and of course I'm coming to the point of catastrophe and chaos?" One must begin there and I believe that with God's help one will definitely be liberated.

"Where sin increased, grace abounded all the more"

As somebody says – and it made a great impression on me – the whole trouble today in society and especially among Christians is this: we believe that evil is more powerful than good. Certainly it may be that we believe in theory that God is more powerful than the devil, that virtue, the grace of God are more powerful than wickedness, than sin, than the activity of Satan, but in practice it appears that we don't believe this.

We see that evil has become so dominant in society – and after what we're saying here, one ascertains that evil has gone all the way inside our existence – so that one wonders: Does the power of good even exist?

What's needed, then – especially right now when we're living through Great Lent and proceeding toward Holy Week and the Resurrection – is for us to believe without the tiniest little doubt that God has the power to redeem us from all that. "Where sin increased, grace abounded all the more."[1] Today where things are so ugly, both outside us, around us, and also within us, more abundant grace will be granted – and abundant grace will be given – by God. And God has the power to free all human beings and make them as He wants them to be.

---

[1] Romans 5: 20.

Chapter Three

Moving Against People

Those Who Consider Others Their Enemies

How one finds his true foundation

We said that since man was created in God's image, he isn't alone, he isn't an individual. Just as God the Father isn't alone. Where the Father is, there also is the Son, there also is the Holy Spirit. The Deity is one, but with respect to persons God isn't a monad but three persons, and in this way there exists a communion of love.

In addition to whatever else it means, as we've said in our previous gatherings, being created in the image of God also means this—that man was not created as one person. He is one man, one humanity, but many persons. And one finds the true purpose in his life, his true foundation, and from there makes a true beginning, precisely when he sees himself together with other human beings.

Today individuality is devouring us. It's something that came from the West, as we've said, and it's something frightful. And day by day, this individualistic spirit enters our country more and more. And while we live in big cities, in large communities, in the end we feel completely isolated. Such is the spirit today that even within the family one feels completely isolated. One doesn't realize from his root, from the depth of his existence, that he is together with others. He doesn't feel this.

Since, therefore, man is in the image of God, he isn't by himself, but is together with others. That's why all the problems that are created come from this root. That is, if one doesn't take a correct position before other people, he certainly won't have a good and smooth development, and some day he'll be blocked inside and come into conflict with other people. Consequently one needs to take the correct position before other people.

And we explained that if a person doesn't take the correct position before other people, he can move toward them in three ways. That is, we have three movements of a person in relation to his fellow human beings. One movement presents itself in some people, another in other people, and the third in others. One of these is that, on account of a lack of true love toward other people, the person moves toward them in a servile manner. We referred to this movement last time and now, before we go any further, let's supplement what we have been saying.

Hanging onto others

Last time we were saying that moving toward others shows that the person feels basically that he can't stand on his own, he can't live by himself. That is, he doesn't have a feeling of self-sufficiency so as to be able to love his fellow-man as a free person, to have communion with him and to feel himself and that person as one man. Two persons but one man. He doesn't have this feeling of self-sufficiency and that's why he hangs onto others in a servile manner and his whole position is such that it doesn't allow him to develop smoothly.

It's possible for a mother or a father to raise their children in such spirit, where the children can't live and can't stand without this hanging onto their parents. Or the contrary can happen – that the parents can't live and stand in life without showing this servility in some way toward their children.

There are parents who lose their sense of self if one day they happen to see their children break away from them for this or that reason, they fall ill and are quite literally overcome by psychosis. And also on the other hand there are children for whom the moment has come for them to get married, to create a family, and they dare not do it. They hesitate. They don't have faith in themselves or in their fellow-man. And most importantly they don't dare to distance themselves from their mother or father or in general from their family environment.

For a person to take before other people – from his earliest years until he grows up, but also when he's fully grown – a position of submission, "captivity," we would say, a position that shows he can't live without them, is something sick. And this position certainly creates painful life-altering experiences, psychic wounds and inner trouble – the blockage, that entanglement we spoke about. And in my humble opinion, it's impossible for this person to have a smooth development, a smooth life, and smooth relations even with those he hangs onto and subjects himself to in a servile manner.

These comments have been made to supplement the discussion of the movement toward people.

With love we situate ourselves correctly before others

We've said that all problems proceed from these three movements a person makes in relation to his fellow-men. Karen Horney mentions these, and I think that theologically and spiritually her position may have a foundation.

She says, then, that one either moves toward people or moves against people or moves away from people. Whatever of the three positions a person has before others, he finds himself in a pathological situation and doesn't have a smooth development. Sometimes a person can have a little of all of them, and that's even worse, because then inside him the movement toward people conflicts with the movement away from people, and it's as if we have someone whom some people pull this way, and others pull him that way to the point that they almost split him in half.

We were saying last time that what protects the person from taking one of these three positions before people is love. He who has learned to love truly will certainly escape from these three traps. And it's important that when the Lord was about to leave His disciples He told them, "By this all men will know that you are My disciples, if you have love for one another."[1] The characteristic mark of this family of Christ was love, true love. Pay attention to that.

Many people talk about love. Today especially, as we realize that the ground is being moved out from under our feet and we're headed for chaos, so much is happening! Both the grown-ups and the young talk about love, they talk about this oneness. But this is a cry which shows exactly the plight of mankind, the sorry state that men have been reduced to as they have left true love behind. Nothing happens merely with words and shouts. What's needed is for man to find true love.

But true love is given only by God, Who came into the world out of love and passed, as we say, through all the stages of life patiently and in the end He was crucified out of love for men and rose from the dead. And He created a group of people to whom again He gave love, and He calls us all to draw near to this group so that we all become one family. When there is true love, then, you have true relations between people, and you escape from these three traps.

We've referred to the slavish movement toward other people. And allow me to remind you of what I said, that it's not only toward other people that slavish, pathological, sick attachment must not exist, but neither must it exist toward

---

[1] John 13:35.

God. And God does not want us in that way. God wants us to be free human beings, and He wants us as free beings to give ourselves absolutely to Him, loving Him, as He, being free, gave Himself to us out of love.

Those who move against others

The second movement is the movement against people. There are more than a few people who are dominated by this trend, who literally suffer from this illness. They consider all people their enemies. They have no inclination to come into substantial dialogue and a relationship of love with others. They have no inclination to work together with others as equals toward equals, just to think, "we are human beings, and they are human beings."

Their tendency and their whole effort is to dominate. Otherwise they can't live, they can't stand in society. In a house, for example, a father who has this tendency can't tolerate it not to dominate there in some way. He can't tolerate it for his wife to say a word to him. He can't have a dialogue with her and from time to time accept her viewpoint: "Yes, you're right. What you say is correct. That's how it must be."

These people always live with the inclination and the tendency to dominate, to conquer, to have their will done. They have continually, as psychology says, a feeling of superiority. That's why they don't find it difficult to behave sadistically, or, for example, to see the other person suffer and not to care less, as long as this tendency of theirs is satisfied. This is their weak point. If this tendency of theirs isn't satisfied, they are the weakest of people, the most insecure of people. And the moment they satisfy this tendency of theirs, it's as if they calm down, as if they are cured. That is, they are like the drug addict who, as soon as he gets his fix, recovers for a while only to rush with more passion to that evil, and subsequently to be much more agitated than he was before he took the narcotic.

Moving against people has this meaning, then, that the person who suffers from this tendency can't be reconciled with people, can't speak in a friendly manner, with love, he can't engage in dialogue, sit down to hear, give way, to submit if need be. He can't agree with others about an issue and work together with them. He reveals himself in a domineering manner, in a conquering manner, in a sadistic manner.

As you can gather, what psychology now comes along and tells us can be grasped very well in a theological and spiritual context. We know how much discussion there is both in the Gospel and by the Church Fathers about this sick condition a person can potentially have, and which can be called egoism. Of course the beginning of every sin is egoism, arrogance, but more particularly in this sadistic tendency, the basis and foundation and first principle is egoism, about which the apostles said so much, and the fathers wrote after them. And they urge a person to submit to any and every sort of sacrifice if he's going to be able to be redeemed from this egoistic tendency, this arrogance, this selfishness he has, so that he can in this way become a real person and so that he himself can find his joy. Because in the end this is the goal.

The more a person denies himself, the more he sacrifices himself, the more he dies to the old man, the more there lives within him the new man, and the more he is a true man. He is the man who finds peace, joy, happiness.

Chapter Four

Moving Away From People

Healthy and Unhealthy Solitude

The basis for man's equilibrium

With God's help in these talks we'll try to go deeper, to make a dive, we could say, into man's soul and to go – from both a psychological and a spiritual viewpoint – as deep as we can go into man, so as to see a few things of which we are unaware but which put us off both psychologically and spiritually.

Remember, we said that the basis of man's equilibrium and consequently the basis of his psychological adjustment, but also particularly his spiritual life and progress is love, love in accordance with God, love in Christ Jesus.

From the very moment of his formation, of his creation, man is made so that he can't exist by himself, but can only exist together with others. And from this beginning of his formation but also from the period of his rebirth, of his re-creation, man exists together with others. Every man is in Adam, and the root of every man is Adam, and somehow we can't exist by ourselves, but all together we are the man whom God created. In the same way, in accordance with the re-creation, in accordance with the re-formation that the Lord achieved every man is in the new Adam, in Christ. We're all together within Christ. There, that is, in Christ, we become true men, we become Christians, as we're united with God – in the person of Christ – and we have a sound relationship and a sound communion with the other human beings. Because of this, the foundation and basis of psychological equilibrium and of man's good spiritual situation and progress is love in Christ; it is this correct communion and contact with the other human beings.

The three pathological movements as a consequence of deviation from love

It's at this point that a person doesn't do well at all, and in the end he realizes that something has occurred inside him, something is happening, something isn't going right inside him as he recognizes that his relations with other people aren't sound, they aren't what they ought to be. That is, if a person – given that he doesn't exist by himself, but together with other people – is finally not able, through love, to take a sound position before others in the world where he lives, one way or the other he'll be crippled in himself, but he'll also be crippled in his relations with others.

If, for example, in his family someone doesn't take a sound position before the other members of the family, or in his work before other people he works with or anywhere else he finds himself, before other people with whom he comes into contact, then not only will he languish, be upset, won't have any inner equilibrium, joy and peace, but he'll also upset others.

For that reason, then – in keeping with what we know from the Church Fathers and in agreement with what certain psychologists say today who help us understand these questions better – as someone deviates from love, by which he has a sound relationship with other people, and which is the foundation of his psychological and spiritual equilibrium, it's possible for him to take one of the following three incorrect positions before others, as we've already said. That is, either to attach himself to others, in which case he kills himself as a personality, or to take a hostile position before other people and find himself in a continuous struggle, in a continuous war, in continuous strife with other people and consequently in a continuous uneasiness and confusion, or to close himself in on himself. We'll speak about this third case now.

Contemporary man enclosed in himself and deprived of true love

Concerning someone who leaves the world and goes and shuts himself in a cave, in a hut, who goes and lives out his life on the cliffs of the Holy Mountain or in some other deserted spot, the prevailing opinion, the prevailing viewpoint is that this man is an egoist, that this man is separating himself from other people, that he is shutting himself inside himself and considering only himself. This viewpoint, however, is mistaken.

Today a great many of those people with whom we come into continuous communication and relationship – both in the home where we live and at our job and in our neighborhood and in various gatherings, as we happen to gather here and now elsewhere – a great many people, among whom we might include ourselves, although they have a great deal of give and take with other people, are probably isolated and don't know it. And perhaps they are of the opinion that the ascetic, the hermit, has taken refuge in the desert thinking and acting egoistically.

Allow me to say that it's not only probable but certain that a great many people in contemporary society are isolated, closed in on themselves. A great many people who live in big and small cities and who continually have good times together, continually come and go together, continually have discussions and profess to fear that by chance they may find themselves alone in some deserted place and may harm society, in the final analysis they're alone, they're closed in themselves and deprived of true love.

It is love, which, in a certain way, opens a door into people's existence and in this way there is communion among them and a mutual give-and-take occurs. In this way a person escapes from the nihilism that his existence has in itself, he escapes from this catastrophe and he can both live and maintain himself in a psychological equilibrium since he has a real relationship with God and with other people, and in this way he can make spiritual progress as well.

A great many people, then, are deprived of this love. And on the one hand, when some of them are deprived of this love, they attach themselves to others. Some are hostile toward others. And yet there are others who aren't hostile toward others – they leave others in peace – nor do they attach themselves to them to any great degree – even though this is somewhat questionable – but they withdraw into themselves, they become enclosed in themselves, they isolate themselves from others and destroy themselves.

This is an unhealthy situation in both psychological and spiritual terms. From what I know and from what I understand, I would say that a great many people – both men and women – suffer from this illness in our days, I would say they are afflicted by it.

The monk's isolation embraces all men

In contrast, the hermit isn't psychologically sick. He who escapes to the cliffs, to the caves, to a cell, or anyway to a secluded monastery doesn't do it because he wants to enclose himself in himself and in this way reduce himself to nothing. He doesn't do it moved by an unhealthy disposition, by the unhealthy inner condition from which contemporary man suffers in the big cities. He does it because he has ascertained, at least for himself, that when he goes there a certain window will open for him, a certain door will open for him, with God's grace and assistance, both toward God and toward other people. And we have such examples, concrete, tangible examples of hermits, ascetics, whose heart opened so wide where they took refuge that not merely do they have room for all men within them, but they actually do have all men within them; and they feel as the Apostle Paul did, who used to say about himself, when he wrote to the Philippians, that he has them within his heart.[1]

And so that we understand one another better, allow me to mention the case of a certain monk, whom I also mentioned at an earlier point. On the Holy Mountain and specifically on the most difficult part of the Holy Mountain, in the place called Karoulia, where the monks use chains to go up and come down and whose diet consists more of wild figs than of bread or other foods, was an ascetic who left the monastery where he was staying and came to that wild place, and he reached such a point of good spiritual condition that he kept praying with tears, many hours in the daytime and many hours at night, for God to take the whole world into paradise even if he himself is to remain outside paradise.[2]

We might not be able to understand what this means. But if we consider that a person who has not only left the world but also his monastery in order to go to a desert to save his soul, in the end he also sacrifices his soul for others, and if we suppose that this person is in his right mind – because even a person who is not in his right mind could do this – if we suppose that this person is thinking rationally, knows what he is seeking, knows what he wants, then we understand what point of holiness, what point

---
[1] See Philippians 1: 7. Compare 2 Corinthians 7:3.
[2] Compare Romans 9: 3: "For I could wish that I myself were accursed and cut off from Christ for the sake of my brethren."

of openness to God's love and openness to other human beings that ascetic has reached. To us who live in the world an unheard-of miracle will have to occur for us to partake of something from this reality of his, to say nothing of reaching the point, the degree of holiness that this man achieved.

Isolation, then, is one thing, closing in on ourselves, running away from others, which is an illness and which is characterized today by psychologists as one of contemporary man's illnesses – from the psychological viewpoint, but why not also from the spiritual viewpoint? – and what the ascetics do, what the hermits do, is another thing, and even what one does who is in the world and tries to live in some way the life of a hermit and an ascetic.

If, then, while we don't have true love, in the end we don't attach ourselves to other people and we aren't hostile toward them, there is a need to examine whether deep down we happen to be very isolated, very closed in on ourselves; if deep down we happen to suffer from what the Fathers call selfishness, which makes us think egoistically, to think only about ourselves; if by any chance we have an unhealthy love, a demonic love, I would say, a love directed toward ourselves.

The reason that many souls have no spiritual progress

Among the people I know there are a great many who believe in God, go to church, receive communion, confess, and who, as they read the Gospel, as they read patristic texts and lives of the saints, they want to progress in the spiritual life; they want to capture and apply parts of these holy lives themselves, something they can experience. In the end, however, they have no success at all.

The facts show that in spite of their desire, in spite of their work and their effort, in spite of the fact that they read this and that, and they listen to this speaker and follow that preacher, in spite of the fact that they act in this way, then, they don't reach the point they want to reach, that they ought to reach, and that they're called to reach. And of course the result, the outcome of this situation is hopelessness, desperation. It's an unconscious conviction created within them that nothing is happening. A conviction that convinces them that nothing of all those things that are written in books ever happened to anyone.

You know, today this wears down the souls of Christians a great deal. Perhaps theoretically and rationally we believe what we read in various spiritual books, but within us, deep in our hearts we have no information, we don't have this certainty that this man really became a saint, that another lived a holy life, that such and such a man, a great sinner really became a great saint, or that a great sinful woman really became a great saint. We don't have this today as a certainty, as a conviction within us.

This faith wears down, then, and one reaches the point at a very deep level, in one's subconscious, of believing that, yes, on the one hand that's what the books say, but it isn't necessarily so. Or one reaches the point – and this is also very common – of excluding oneself from the matter. That is, he believes more or less that God performed this miracle for everybody else, but he begins to believe, he begins to be persuaded that this miracle can't take place for him.

As we've said, while a person believes in God, makes the effort, struggles, reads, receives communion, confesses, and sees no progress whatsoever, he reaches the point of persuading himself about this: "It's okay for people of other times or for other people who are living today, but for me there is no progress, for me there is no hope of this miracle taking place" – the miracle that Christ came to perform in all human beings and in each one separately, and consequently in him. And so, while the person has this reservation deep in the subconscious or even in the unconscious, while he has this doubt or this conviction with respect to himself – allow me to say it – the door of his soul, the window of his soul, through which God's grace will pass, which will free him, which will raise him up and will make him a spiritual person, is completely closed.

To such a person who really isn't deceiving himself, but is struggling spiritually and really doing something, but in the end doesn't reach the point he's called to reach and that he ought to reach, personally I believe that something of the sort must happen. That is, as the person doesn't have true love within him, he moves toward others in a mistaken manner: Either he attaches himself to some person or persons, or disposes himself in a hostile manner towards other people, or his existence is closed off before others, he's isolated from others, and within him, within his existence there nestles that selfishness, there nestles that giving to himself and not the openness toward others. This is something which, from what I know, someone can have, can live, can be led about here and there by it and can be a victim of this deeper reality which exists within him, and in spite of all that he may not suspect its existence.

And this is the reason that even at this moment that we are hearing these words, we are all hearing them, but probably none of the things we're saying reaches the door of this unhealthy condition in order to draw away from there a curtain that covers this reality and to make this unhealthy condition appear before our eyes in the harshest terms; and in this way to cause someone to decide to seek therapy and finally to be healed, to be cured, and consequently to be freed from this illness. And so afterwards to see his desire, his love, his effort and his struggle, take his reading and what he hears and sees, if you allow me, so that all these things bear fruit within his existence.

Hypocritical cultivation of the soul

Surely you must have read or heard that the elders in those ancient years – Antony the Great, Paul the Simple, St. Pachomios and the other holy Desert Fathers – used to test their disciples.

He who is going to go to the desert will either go crazy – if he doesn't take the correct position he should take where he has gone – or he'll become a holy man. Because in that place there is no such atmosphere to help him be attached or to contribute to his taking a hostile position toward others or which will cause him to close in on himself. In that place, his soul is like an open book both before God and before his elder.

Today, however, such is in general the whole spirit of society, of contemporary Christian society, which promotes in good Christians – those of us who consider ourselves good Christians; we aren't speaking about other people – a hypocritical stance, a hypocritical situation and cultivation of the soul. And so while one attaches himself to some elder, a thing which at depth is not merely a sickness but also a sin, this is considered a virtue.

In the eyes of St. Antony, in the eyes of St. Paul, of St. Pachomios, of St. Basil and the other Neptic Fathers, it would have been immediately noticeable that not only is this not a virtue, but that it's a sin and an unhealthy situation, and they would have taken appropriate actions. Today, however, things are so mixed up that something which deep down is a sickness and consequently also a sin – since it alienates man from love, from the true love of God and makes him selfish – is considered a virtue.

So also on the other hand, one who is isolated, a person who is closed off, one who turns toward himself and drowns himself inside there, is probably considered an ascetic type, a hesychastic type, a mystic and generally speaking a very spiritual person, while deep down this person is not merely committing sin, but his whole condition is unhealthy. It's a manifestation of a sometimes deeper and a sometimes milder illness.

Why we don't manage to understand one another

There's a need, then, for Christians of our days to pay attention to this third point: While they supposedly avoid attaching themselves to others or while they deep down supposedly avoid getting into conflicts with others, can it be that they are at that moment pushing their souls deeper into that closure, into that death that's hidden within themselves?

Allow me to say here that the following strange thing happens: The person who closes himself in on himself attaches himself as well. And this, as a rule, is because the person who closes himself in himself – like the other who attaches himself – is a person who can't live by himself. He's a person who has a dependency on others in spite of his being closed in himself. He has a dependency in spite of the fact that he draws back into himself and perhaps he has no companionship with others or even avoids talking with them. That's why we have this paradox: The person who avoids others so much that we would say that the only thing left for him to do is to get up and go to the monastery since he cannot get along with others, doesn't dare go. Why? Because there's no place for that sort of thing there, that is, for the fact that at the same time he wants to rely on something, at the same time he wants to be dependent.

Certainly if this is how things are, this is how they are. They can't change suddenly. A person isn't set right with a stroke of the pen. The worst thing – as I emphasize so many times – is for one to be unaware of his situation and to consider his illness, his sin – if I may put it that way – as a virtue, and to make others consider it a virtue as well. This is very bad.

One must know oneself: "I'm a poor little creature and I can't make it on my own. I certainly want someone to rely on. While I want this, however, on the other hand I can't make a commitment to work together with the other person fully and openly. I also want to have my little self, I also want to be a little autonomous, by myself." When one knows this, then, he'll say, "I'm a little guy." And he'll beseech God, he'll also go to find a suitable person who can help him, and he will do whatever else is required so as slowly, a little bit at a time, to free himself from this condition and make progress toward a healthy condition, to make progress toward the truth. When a person does not recognize this, however, then things are very bad, both for him and for those around him.

And allow me to say that all the unpleasant things that happen, the dramas, if you want me to speak in this way, all that difficulty that is presented in Christian families, in Christian groups, generally among Christians, and which makes life difficult, all these things come precisely from the fact that ordinary Christians, too, are not only sick deep inside – something isn't right with them – but furthermore they are unaware of it, they don't know it, and that's why each one wants to try and impose his own sick condition on the other; he wants and tries to make the other person conform and agree with his own unhealthy disposition and with his own unhealthy opinion.

Of course the other also has his own unwell situation, and so a conflict is created, strife, war, struggle, there's misunderstanding and in the end good Christians don't manage to understand one another and work together. Good Christians don't manage to live together. Each one has his "religion," each one has his "god," each one worships God as he thinks best, and Christians don't feel deep down – because the love about which we spoke is absent – that they are really brothers, that they are really one human being. A human being who comes from the first Adam and from the second Adam, Jesus Christ.

Why Does One Close Oneself up in an Unhealthy Way?

The whole question in this life is for a person – rooted in Christ – to be able to develop together with the rest of the people around him as a distinct personality and not to get tangled up with other personalities.

Remember, our starting point was Orthodox theology and the faith that God is Trinitarian. The Orthodox Church has fought a great struggle over this issue. The Father is the Father, the Son is the Son. The Father is never the Son, the Son is never the Father. The Holy Spirit is the Holy Spirit. He is never the Father or the Son. The Deity is one, but the persons are distinct. They are never identical.

Let's come to man now. We all belong to one humanity, to one human race, to one man. And this one man is Christ. However, as man was created in God's image, we are distinct persons. And we said that all man's problems are created because we confront this reality incorrectly. That holds true even for small children.

A last defense

When we don't help a little child to develop as a distinct person, then either he will subordinate himself pathologically to others, or he'll take a hostile stance before others, or he'll be closed in on himself. This closing in on himself isn't accidental. It's certainly an illness, but at the same time it's also a defense. We could say that it's an effort the person makes – here, the child – so that people don't rob him of his personality, so that they don't dismantle it, so that they don't destroy his personality. Because really, just as we don't know how to live in this society, even in our families, the mother's stance, and generally the stance and actions of parents toward children can often be dismantling of a child's personality. Personality, however – which is given from God and is the root and structure of each person's existence – isn't easily surrendered, it isn't easily dismantled. And in its effort not to be dismantled, each personality acts this way or that – in one of the three ways we mentioned. Of course, the way it acts is pathological, it's unhealthy, it's outside the correct manner of confronting things. The fact is, in any case, that the personality isn't easily surrendered.

The moment that someone subordinates himself in a pathological manner, that he subjugates himself – like the child who in the end subordinates himself to his mother in a slavish way, in a pathological way, and by his action his personality appears to be destroyed, and so it is – at that moment he's using a defensive weapon he has inside him to keep his personality from being completely dismantled. That is, it's as if the child says, "I can't take it anymore. My mother and the others are conducting themselves toward me in such a manner that I won't be able to bear it in any other way unless I bow my head in order to save what I can." If I am allowed to say it, he acts like the captive who pretends to become a submissive instrument of those who took him captive and willingly does one thing and another until he finds a suitable opportunity to escape, to be liberated.

The moment, then, that the personality subordinates itself slavishly – since it cannot bear it any longer – at that moment it uses the last defensive weapon it has in order to hold onto something of itself. And also at the moment that it conducts itself with hostility towards other human beings, it uses a defensive weapon. But above all, we would say, the moment that someone is closed in on himself, he uses this as a defensive weapon because he has seen and understood that there's no other way for him to save himself. It's now another matter altogether that he doesn't see things correctly. In any case, however, that's the way he sees things, the way he judges things – these things of course happen subconsciously and instinctively. He sees other people in some way as rapacious beings who want to take from him not merely his belongings – his clothes or his money or I don't know what else – but his very existence. They want to dismantle his existence.

So then he closes himself off, he barricades himself in himself. He can carry on a discussion, he can do this and that, he can even subordinate himself as it was said, but in the end he doesn't let anyone into his existence. In the end his existence doesn't open up to other human beings. It's another thing altogether that this is annihilation, it is the destruction of the human being. But I'm explaining why someone does it. Yes, he does it precisely in order to preserve his personality.

How is the personality preserved?

In the end, however, the human being's personality is preserved by love. Normally one resists the no-good influences of others and comes "to mature manhood, to the measure of the stature of the fullness of Christ"[1] by the love we've spoken about. Love is what helps the personality to avoid being tangled up with other personalities. In Christianity that's the way things are.

The following has now come to my mind. According to ancient philosophy, according to neo-Platonism and according to nirvana, if you will, human beings are identified with God. According to Buddhist philosophy, every human

---

1 Ephesians 4: 13.

being in relation to God resembles a droplet that has been splashed from a river. Let's say a river flows along in a rush and as it encounters rocks and, in general, uneven ground, droplets of water are tossed up. But these droplets fall back into the river and in this way they become one with the river as they were from the beginning. The men of this religion believe that man's relationship with God is like this. And according to neo-Platonism the matter is somewhat the same. That is, in the end the human being – according to them – returns to God and is identified with God, becomes one with God.

According to the Gospel, according to Orthodox Christian teaching, man is forever a distinct being. And only a distinct being can love and accept love. True love never identifies us with the other, but neither does it ever distance us from the other.

True love maintains and preserves the personality in such a way that it isn't mingled together, it isn't identified with other personalities – not even with God. But true love also takes the personality out of itself and brings it into true communion with other personalities, and so it isn't reduced to nothing, it doesn't die within itself. Because whenever a being, a created thing, is closed in on itself, in the end it dies. This is what nothingness is, which, today the existentialist philosophy of nothingness teaches.

In the end, certainly, just as these people teach and just as they say, man really does end up at nothing, he ends up at death, and the reason is that he isn't open toward God and toward other human beings through the love that springs from Christ, and in this way he dies inside himself. Or he can consort with others and in this way again he dies. And that's why the existentialist philosophers of nothingness say that hell is other people. This is an error. Paradise is other people – in the following sense. When human beings live in Christ, when they feel God's grace inside them, then a communion of love exists among persons as there exists among the persons of the Holy Trinity, in conformity with what the Lord said: "That they also may be one in Us" and "That they may be one just as We are one."[2] Within this reality, the others are, we could say, paradise.

And so when someone subordinates himself and when he takes a hostile stance before others, but also when he is closed in on himself, he does it because he wants to preserve himself. That is, it's as if someone says, "Even if I'm going to be psychologically ill, even if I won't be a normal and sound human being, at least my deepest existence will be preserved." But these are pathological conditions.

However, when this human being who has such an unhealthy condition understands how he himself is, deep down, and how he moves, and he can be given truly to Christ and truly be reborn in Christ, then he'll really be flooded with love, he'll become a true personality and will have a true, real relationship with other human beings.

---

2 John 17: 21-2.

Far from Themselves

Something we're compelled to do

We'll make reference again to those who are distanced from other people.

In our times, in the period we're now living, life – the way of life, society, the mindset, the spirit that exists and civilization in general – is such that it draws every human being out of himself, diffuses him outwardly, scatters him, causes him to be diverted. That's why more than ever before, in our years, in our times people need to distance themselves from time to time from others, to be with themselves and to discuss, to engage in dialogue with themselves.

And it's true that quite a few people do this. Not only do people who believe in Christ and struggle to be good Christians try very often to withdraw to be with God and engage in this dialogue with themselves, but others do it, too, moved simply by a philosophical disposition, for self-improvement, to help their inner selves to be guided to an inner fullness. And that's not a bad thing. It is rather imperative that it happen, especially – I repeat – in our times.

Alienated from others

In spite of the fact, however, that people today are continuously with others, yet there are people who live constantly far from others whether or not they are among others, whether or not they live in a family that has other members, too, or whether they work at a job – in a factory or in a store – and have co-workers, employees, colleagues. They are among other people, they live together with others, yet they live far from others, alienated from others. And in fact perhaps they have never bent down deeper into themselves to engage in a true dialogue with themselves. Although they are constantly with themselves, since they constantly avoid others and are constantly separated from others, in the end they don't penetrate into the knowledge of themselves and they don't engage in this dialogue with themselves.

However, those who are separated from others aren't the only ones who, in a unhealthy manner, certainly, love this distancing, this alienation. The other two categories of people we talked about are also separated from others.

That is, when one attaches himself to people, as we were saying, in the final analysis he doesn't have true communication and he doesn't find himself in a true relationship with them, he doesn't have true love toward them. And that one also who takes a hostile stance before people and continually quarrels, gets upset, fights with them, certainly has a certain relationship with them – he isn't alienated from them – but essentially he's separated from people.

Especially, though, this type who, as we said, moves away from people, especially him, in the end he moves away from himself as well. This type doesn't know his real self. Although he's continuously with himself, although he's closed off, barricaded, entrenched in himself and takes all the necessary steps so that others don't have a chance to approach him psychically, that is, so that he does not have a chance to come into psychic contact with people, in the end he doesn't know who he is, what he believes, what he hopes, what he fears. He finds himself in such a situation that he isn't merely alienated from others, but he's even alienated from himself as well and in the end he doesn't know himself. Of course, the other types – though from a different perspective – don't know themselves.

The need for self-sufficiency

Well, it's as if this type is creating an enclosing wall around himself and up to a point – up to this wall, up to this trench – he allows others to approach him. From that point on he'll do everything he can do to prevent anyone from coming even a little further into his existence, lest any communication ensue.

And so the very first need this person feels, this unhealthy type, is to have some self-sufficiency. Since he's isolated, since he doesn't cooperate, he doesn't communicate with others, since he has no give and take with others, it's natural for him to do everything he can so that he can cope with things by himself. Consequently he does everything to be self-sufficient, to have self-sufficiency. A fellow of that sort amazes people sometimes by his resourcefulness. That is, he amazes them because of his capacity to find solutions in his ordinary daily life among other people.

Regular people, who aren't unhealthy – if we suppose that people exist today who aren't unhealthy, because, as we've said, everybody is more or less affected by this illness we're speaking about, or by the others – in any case, those who are somewhat free from illness in some way, can't consider certain things, can't conceive certain things which he will consider, he will conceive, he will contrive, who has precisely this need to be self-sufficient, to have self-sufficiency. What does it mean to have self-sufficiency? It means for a person to be able to live by himself.

All people more or less have a need of others. A normal person has no problem in asking for the help of others and in allowing himself to depend a little on them. A normal person has no problem helping others and having them help him, obligating others in his way and being obligated. An abnormal person, however, the type we are discussing, as soon as he sees that something is going to happen that will pressure him in some way, to have a need of some person, that will compel him to be obligated to this person, to have a dependency on him, he immediately gathers himself into his shell and remains there alone.

Closed in even before God

This type is the person who constantly needs solitude. He needs solitude so much that even before God – and please, let's pay special attention to this – he's afraid to open up. That is, even before God he wants to remain alone. He is terrified of the truth that God sees everything and knows everything, that nothing escapes God and God's eye. This reality, this truth terrifies him, that is, that it's possible for God's glance to fall inside his hiding place, inside his solitude, inside his shell, inside this confinement of his, and it's possible for God to know this, and to know that.

Do you want us to go a little further? Not merely does it terrify him that God's eye sees all things, that God's mind knows this and that, but, just as his existence is closed in, he doesn't want anyone to pass inside this enclosure, inside this wall, except himself. This is frightful, it's terrifying if it's true – and it *is* true. And it can happen to many people, particularly to people who are Christians, to people who have a relationship with God, with the Church, who have a relationship with people, with other Christians – but all those things up to a point. From that point on don't let anyone – whether some Christian or especially some priest or even God Himself – come further into the soul.

This type, then, is the sort of person who can't open himself to God, who can't trust in God. He ends up being that Christian who is doing fine, just fine, but deep down – he feels it, he sees it, when he's paying attention – he still doesn't have communion with God, he still doesn't have contact with God. The light of God hasn't come into this secret darkness that exists inside him, into this double-locked shell of his. And he has a consciousness of this reality – if it's certain that he has it, but he may not have it. And sometimes one asks oneself: Why, after all, while he believes up to a point, while he struggles to be a Christian, while he carries out a lot of Christian duties and wants to have communion with God, in the end, he doesn't have it? He wonders why. Or he wonders why he doesn't love other Christians, why he doesn't love other people. It's possible that the whole relationship between this "good" Christian and other people appears to be good, it may be ongoing, but at depth, however, his existence has no communion with other people, and this Christian doesn't feel that the other existences pass into him and his own existence passes into the other existences. That is, he doesn't perceive his soul to be open so that the love of his brothers, his fellow Christians, and first and foremost the love of God passes inside him.

A situation that is difficult to get rid of

This situation is unhealthy and, you know, it's a difficult thing for it to go away. It's possible that we say repeatedly that it must go away, it's possible that we want it to go away and we try to make it go away, and yet it may not go away.

Let me give you an example so that you understand. It's as difficult for granite to melt from an ordinary fire as for this situation to be resolved by ordinary efforts. In order for granite to melt, it requires a very high temperature. And in order for this situation to go away, for this wall to melt and the soul to open, it requires, to be sure, a great temperature of faith.

What is required first of all, I think, is for one to understand things in this way, to see them in this way, to accept that this is how things are, and to make a decision about this granite, this rock, this hardness that has been established inside him and which distances his soul from God and from people – to set it down into God's fire. This, however, is exactly what that type doesn't want to do.

But as soon as one understands it, he must say, "Whether I want to or not, it has to happen." And if he begins acting in that way, sooner or later God's fire will melt this hardness, God will enter his soul, heaven will open, and he will become a Christian and will taste this new life. Then he won't just hear about Christians and the Christian life, but he'll know within him more fully what "Christian" means and how a Christian lives.

Closed off in a Compulsive Way

Our topic is that type who seeks independence, isolation, who seeks solitude.

Personally I believe that a person is what he is from his birth, but he also becomes what he becomes as he lives in society. We've said that so many times and we must emphasize it once again, each of us has a certain sort of disposition from birth, of one sort or another, each has certain points of departure, each has a specific personality. And then along come our parents, our teachers, the neighborhood, and generally speaking the environment, life's events, life's adversities, and all these things make their contribution so that in the end our character is shaped and in this way we belong to a certain type.

And some may belong to that type of person who is attached to others, who depends on others and who can't live without this dependence. Everything is lost for him if, let's suppose, he remains without dependence. Others may belong to that type that considers everybody their enemy. He quarrels with everybody and can't discern in anybody a disposition of goodness, of love, a disposition of cooperation. They are all his enemies, they are all dangerous and he has to take a defensive position toward all of them. Yet others may belong to the third type, which seeks independence, isolation, solitude. It's certainly possible that I am led astray in the way I'm putting things, but it seems to me that what I am saying is true.

He's afraid open up

From what I know, from the little experience I have, this type that distances himself from people can be a religious person – he can read the Gospel, go to church, partake of the mysteries of the Church – he can appear pious, sometimes even be considered a saint, and yet in the depth of his existence God's grace may not have approached him at all, in the depth of his existence there may not have yet appeared a ray of God's light. And this because he's very closed off, well fenced in or enclosed. For him it's a catastrophe to open up. We could say that this type knows one word – closed. Openness frightens him – and still more openness before God.

That's why we sometimes say in sermons and other homilies that the whole question is for a person to be opened up to the grace of God, to be opened up to God's light. But this means that a person surrenders fully to God, this means that he accepts a visitor within him. He stops being fenced in and closed off. The unhealthy type, however, can't do this, because he seeks isolation, he has recourse to isolation in a compulsive way.

And here's the big problem. This is why in other respects someone can be very religious, very pious, he can study the Gospel a great deal, be a man of the Church, but all the same if he belongs to this unhealthy type, whether he wants to or not, whether understands it or not, in a compulsive way he remains closed off. And outside this enclosure, outside this depth of his existence, a hyper-sensitivity is created in a certain way, like a defense mechanism, which is immediately set in motion, at work, in operation, as soon as something comes along and influences this soul at its depth, as soon as it comes along in some way to obligate this soul to do something (against its will) or as soon as it gives the appearance that it wants to oppress this soul.

Some characteristics of the person who isolates himself

As the experts say, precisely because these people attach great importance to this inner freedom and to not losing their freedom, their independence, their solitude, they even reach the point that even completely external things bother them. For example, if their shoes pinch them, their belt, their necktie, this bothers them. If they find themselves in a place which is obstructed in front somehow and they can't see, this, too, bothers them. Or, if they find themselves in a closed space, in a tunnel, in a gallery, on an underground road, they can't stand it. Or, it bothers them a great deal, it annoys them, when they are going to assume a long-term obligation (for example, when they are going to make a contract, when they are going to get married).

We don't know what degree some people who remain unmarried fail to move toward marriage because God calls them to another life. It may be that they remain unmarried because they are afraid of marriage. They think they'll lose this freedom – this unhealthy freedom, however. They think they'll lose this independence – this unhealthy independence, of course. To be precise, they're afraid that someone else will enter the depths of their existence, and they don't want this at all. Certainly other needs exist that finally cause them to get married. For example, when a woman is looking for protection, affection, in the end she'll get married, but this shortcoming will exist. How is a communion of souls and persons possible in this marriage, then? In the same way, but from the other side, the side of men, the same thing can occur, and so there is no way then to have communication of souls.

It's possible for these sick types to do a few things which appear at first sight to be small and without great importance, but for them these are steps they take for their freedom to be preserved. For example, if someone is obligated to go to his job at eight – at the shop or the office where he's an employee – he thinks he's being harmed inside if he goes exactly at eight. He'll go at one minute past eight, two minutes past eight, five minutes past eight. And he does this so as to feel he's preserving his freedom this way. This person can offer a lot to others, he can attend to others and help them, but as soon as others make a specific request of him, he doesn't do it. And that happens because he feels as if he's tied up, as if he's bound, as if he's being depended on. He can take some gift to a fellow human being, for example, to an acquaintance of his, if the other person isn't expecting it. If he's expecting it, he doesn't take it to him.

This is the person who wants his life to be an exception. He doesn't live as others live. He wants to do something special, something different. He feels that he's getting lost as soon as he enters the regular life where everybody else lives. That is, he thinks he's losing this very freedom of his, this independence of his.

This is the person who particularly aims at superiority. The first type, the compliant one, the attached one, seeks superiority, too, and the other who quarrels with everyone seeks it as well, but we could say that this last type seeks it much more. He's the one who, more than all the others, rests in this feeling of superiority because he's always alone, independent, he's always closed in on himself. How can he stand on his feet, how can he be supported somehow, feel comfortable somehow, if he doesn't have the idea that he's a genius, that he himself has a special value, that he's something great? This nourishes him, it satisfies him, it relaxes him, it pleases him. He is made to look completely ridiculous, however, when life's events and situations contradict him.

Because, you know, it doesn't matter what idea, what opinion we have about ourselves, what we think we are. Life is a reality and, whether we like it or not, at a certain moment it forces us to come down to earth. As that is happening that man sees finally that he isn't a genius at all, that he doesn't have a special value, that he himself isn't something he can rely on. And in such circumstances, it's as if he were turning into someone unrecognizable, as if he were no longer the man he appeared to be. He takes refuge – ridiculed, of course – in others and seeks protection, affection, love. Certainly he takes steps again and again so that no one enters the depth of his existence, so that in the end he remains alone again. Because that's the greatest danger and the greatest disaster for him – that someone might happen to enter his walled tower, this secure hiding-place.

While he's seeking superiority he doesn't engage in a competition with other people, he doesn't compete with them. He believes, however, that his whole existence deep inside is a great treasure, and he expects others to see this treasure and recognize him. He expects them to see his worth. That is the person who – as Karen Horney says – imagines himself as a solitary tree on some hilltop, and all the other people are like trees on the sides of the hill, none of which stand out. They are all the same. He's the only tree that is on the hilltop and stands out.

With confidence in God's hands

How is it possible, my brothers, for God's grace to enter such a soul at a moment when it's living in an unhealthy way? "In an unhealthy way" means, among other things, that whether someone wants to or not, somehow this is how he's living in the depth of his existence. How is it possible for such a soul to receive grace? How is it possible for the light of Christ to come to such a soul? It isn't possible. And this person can be religious for his whole lifetime, he can struggle in a way he thinks is best, and in the end, deep down his very self is uncultivated and unhealthy and God's grace hasn't visited it at all.

However, regardless of how things are, if the person begins to understand what's happening to him a little at a time and he makes a decision to begin to humble himself before God and to try to exercise a little courage to release himself with confidence into God's hands, God will find a way to enter this person's very own dark basement, into his own dark and hard soul, and transform his existence and make him a true man, a true Christian.

And then he'll also see other people as true human beings and will have true contact and true communion with them. And of course one will have come to the road of salvation and will proceed from progress to progress, from grace to grace, until he is perfected in Christ Jesus.

The Type that Moves within Negativity

The one who deadens his feelings

In this section of our talks we're dealing with the type who aims at isolation, who wants to withdraw from others, to flee, to distance himself from others. He's a type who moves within negativity. One would say that the other two types move in affirmation. This one, however, moves only in negativity. He doesn't want people to approach him, he doesn't want them to influence him, he doesn't want them to obligate him to do anything.

This type also has the tendency, among other things, to deaden his feelings, to suspend them, not to allow them to act, to operate. And he does this, as a rule, because every one of our feelings, this or that feeling, causes us to open up, to express ourselves, causes us to manifest ourselves. Precisely because this type of person is closed, however – closed off even before his very self, we would say – when this type takes up relations with other people, when he comes into social interactions with them, when he allows himself to express his feelings a little bit toward others and to accept the feelings of others, he's afraid he'll be betrayed. He's afraid that something will spring forth from his deepest existence and break through that barrier, that wall that exists between him and others. He's afraid that some window or other will open and in that way his existence will be betrayed – something he doesn't want on any account.

Precisely on account of the fact that he's closed off, precisely on account of this entrenchment of his, even when he understands that something isn't going well inside himself and he tries to find help from someone he thinks can help him, this type can sit for hours chatting with the person from whom he wants help, but deep down, he remains barricaded, closed off. He spends hours discussing whatever is outside this wall he has created around himself, he talks about it, he keeps on talking about it. But he takes all possible steps to avoid changing himself in any basic sense – in spite of the fact that this specific effort is taking place – so that his personality will remain what it is.

It's as if a chasm is gaping, opening up before him, if, even for a moment, he thinks that his personality can stop being what it was up to now and change and become something else. He thinks a chasm is opening before him simply because he has this thought. That's why, in the end, he remains again closed off. Deep down, in the hidden recesses of his existence, he still remains unchanged, without alteration, although he can become tired and even wear others out as he seeks help and discusses his problem.

He wants to preserve his freedom

This is certainly no accident, that is, when someone closes himself off and doesn't allow anyone to come inside him. This is no accident. Let's explain it. Remember, we were saying last year and the year before that every human being who comes into this world has a consciousness of his existence, of his being, of his ego. Every human being who comes into this world is a person. And it's given by God for someone to do everything to preserve his personality, his ego – in the good sense – his freedom. What's happening in this case?

As a person grows up from childhood, he confronts various difficulties, he accepts various onslaughts in life. And when he doesn't know the appropriate way to confront all these things, and he's going to protect himself and in this way preserve his personality, he's led precisely to this unwholesome situation we're talking about – from that point on he closes himself off in himself. While his first principle is that he must save himself, his good self, his real self, in the end a sickness sets in, an unhealthy condition, the fact that he's closed off in himself. And this closure is unavoidably a compulsive action in the sense that he's incapable of acting differently.

In any case, I'd like to say this in closing. You see, God made man free and put him in paradise. What does it mean to say that He made him free? It means that God made him pure, clean, with a natural and spontaneous inner tendency toward good, toward God. But man also had the potential to say no to God and to take the other path which in fact is what he did.

God respects this thing, this freedom. God honored it not only when He made man free, but still today when man is sinful, fallen, God still respects his freedom. And if a human being is to be saved, God wants him free. That is, He wants man to want to be saved freely, to want to come to God freely, to submit himself to God freely, and to remain free and to live as a man of God, free.

This is something basic. And this, we would say, is the first and most important principle, even in this type who withdraws, who isolates himself and ends up in an unwholesome condition. He too starts from this point – from the fact that he wants to preserve his freedom. In a basic sense this is certainly good, but for many different reasons, in the end he is led to this sick condition. But we'll return to this topic.

Unpleasant Consequences of Opening up to Others

Untouched as a person and at the same time in communion with others

In our previous talk we said that this type that prefers solitude, isolation, who distances himself from people, who moves away from people in a way, also acts this way because, among other things, he wants to preserve his personality, he wants to preserve his deepest being.

And the whole mistake is precisely in this. Whereas man was fashioned by God and re-fashioned by Christ in such a way as to preserve his personhood in one piece and at the same time to be completely in communion – certainly in God – with other human beings, the type that moves away from people doesn't succeed in this. He thinks – or that's the way it can possibly happen – that exactly at the moment that he comes into communion with other people, he loses his personhood, his personality. I have a few such cases in mind.

People who are closed off, internally isolated, discontent, wronged – that is, people who consider themselves wronged by others – people who hadn't found affection, love, not even in their families – from their father, from their mother – when they grew up they cultivated the tactic of isolating themselves as much as they could and withdrew within themselves. And when some person turns up in their lives – in the case of a girl, when a boy turned up, and in the case of a boy, if a girl turned up – who in their manner and their behavior, with their words, whether they were phony, hypocritical or not, had managed to unlock their soul, to open a door in the wall in which their soul was enclosed, and afterwards this person had been proven to be a liar, then a disaster took place.

Once in its life this soul decided to open up, to come into communion with another person, and it was burned more than it could bear. This happened, not only because it was deceived, cheated, but also because it didn't know how to remain untouched as a person and at the same time come into communion with other human beings. Here is the point of great delicacy, and it's extremely difficult to reconcile these two things.

Nervous breakdown

I'm going back to where I started. That person who moves away from people is right, up to a certain point, to barricade himself, to draw back. He's justified up to a certain point to be very cautious. However, this withdrawal, this solitude, this isolation goes too far and from that point on it's an unwholesome situation. It's not a healthy situation, as in the case of the monk who leaves the world and everything and can remain all alone even for fifty years. The monk doesn't do this moved by an unwholesome disposition. That's why even there where he's all by himself, his soul is open to every human being. He has no difficulty on this point so as not to be able to come into communion with others. Nor does he feel like his personality is being destroyed when he comes into communion with others, so as consequently to withdraw for that reason. No. He doesn't withdraw for that reason. On the contrary, the type we're talking about withdraws precisely for this reason.

And when this type is compelled by a given situation to remain a little with other people, to associate a little with them, to come into some communication with them, that is, to emerge from his shell, then he suffers what we call a nervous breakdown, as he finds himself in unfamiliar waters, he loses his security. The result is that one person can be driven to drink and end up an alcoholic, another can reach the point of trying to kill himself, or another can have morbid, neurotic symptoms. And one reaches this point when he's provoked in some way and compelled to emerge from his shell. And since he can't tolerate that, he suffers a nervous breakdown.

Of course the nervous breakdown that takes place in certain souls can appear to the eyes of those souls as being due to certain specific reasons. Allow me to refer to a few examples. As soon as a woman discovers that her husband is lying to her about certain matters, she suffers a nervous breakdown. When someone expects something from his boss and his request isn't accepted, he reaches the point of suffering a nervous breakdown.

Little events of this type can lead this person who seeks solitude to a nervous breakdown. And while the reason that provokes the nervous breakdown may be deeper, may be, in fact, this very moving away from people, all the same, both the person himself who suffers and those around him who see him, attribute the nervous breakdown to external events. Sometimes even psychiatrists are led astray. That is, they think the nervous breakdown comes from the little event, from this insignificant occurrence.

It can be, let's say, that one has before him a person who says that he isn't doing too well. "Why aren't you doing well?" he asks him. "Because a few days ago," he replies, "this and that happened to me." And as we study what he refers to, we see that it isn't possible to get that result from that little occurrence – that is, for the person to suffer a nervous breakdown, to find himself in unfamiliar waters, to go out of his senses, to experience neurosis or even psychosis. This isn't warranted.

In these circumstances we have to search deeper to see what's happening. Then we'll discover exactly what the root of the illness is, and the root is this – the person who is withdrawn into himself, this type who is isolated, closed off, he has his security in there. Inside this tower of his, inside this fortress he feels secure. And when he's compelled by a given situation to emerge, then he loses his sense of who he is. That is, there is a certain context to the matter.

The person who is closed off, when he's compelled by a certain situation, in a way to emerge from himself, or when he's compelled to permit things to get into his inner being, he's terrified, he's overcome by panic, he feels that this fortress in which he was safe is being destroyed. And what's worse, he's overcome by fears. He thinks his personality is being completely destroyed, he thinks that he'll be lost inside the chaos of other human beings and he'll lose his uniqueness – because all of us have more or less this impression that we're something unique, and this is true up to a certain point. This person reaches the point of being afraid of many things, but most of all he's afraid that he'll go crazy. Not that he'll lose his mind, but that he'll become completely disorganized, that he'll split apart, that his personality will be dismantled. It is something very frightening.

And all these things happen precisely because this person very deeply – who knows for certain when all this started? – didn't learn to come into normal, true communion with other people and to confront life's events correctly. He learned only one thing – to run away. To run away from people, to run away from events. From all those things which he felt are enemies, which try to come to destroy his personality.

And the whole secret is here – the person who is reborn in Christ Jesus – is really reborn, he's reborn from his roots, from the depths of his existence, his personhood itself is reborn, and he doesn't merely perform a few religious duties or have a few Christian habits – this person not only maintains his personality unharmed, but also just as true love works, he comfortably comes into contact with other people, and confronts with ease all those things he's going to encounter in life. He struggles, he is hurt, he gets tired, but in the end, he conquers.

If, a little at a time, a human being begins to understand what's happening to him and makes a decision to begin to humble himself before God and to try to take a little courage to let himself go with faith into God's hands, God will find a way to enter his dark basement, his dark and hard soul, and to transform his existence and make him a true human being, a true Christian.

The whole question is for a person to be opened up to the grace of God. But this means that the person surrenders fully to God, this means that he accepts a visitor within him. He ceases to be barricaded and closed. The unhealthy type, however, can't do this, because he seeks isolation, he has recourse to isolation in a compulsive way.

Salvation is given for free and it's extremely easy. But people get things mixed up and seek salvation elsewhere, since deep inside resides the ego, there resides selfishness. There resides this love of ourselves, which begins from the day that the first-created fell. With the fall, that is, the first-created stopped looking to God and began to look to themselves; they turned toward themselves.

Chapter Five

The Idealized Image

Identifying with a Fantasy

A general reference

We're about to enter a new chapter to which I give altogether special importance. We'll be speaking about the idealized image. Based on some experience I have, I think we all suffer from this, and we "good" Christians suffer from it even more. But what do we mean by the "idealized image"?

Every human being, apart from what he really is, desires to be something more, he desires to reach a certain point. So he shapes a good, ideal, idealized image, as it's said, for himself. The bad thing is that the neurotic type – and let me say that to a greater or lesser extent this germ exists in all of us, that to a greater or lesser extent we all belong to this type – as he relies on this image he has created for himself, he thinks that he is already this image. And so he leaves behind the reality he is and passes over to this imaginary condition. That is, his real self is one thing while he thinks he is something else, since he has been gripped by an idealized image and for evermore he thinks this imaginary image is his self. And although the idealized image isn't reality, it exists inside him and influences him. In fact, most often this image has a flattering character. It finds pleasure in flattering the one who created it and it wants to be liked by him.

Please don't misunderstand me about what I am going to say next. A certain newspaper had published a cartoon. It presented a lady who was chubby and rather old, looking into a mirror. And in the mirror the cartoonist made the lady as she was imagining herself to be. In the mirror she was thin and young, this chubby old lady. That's how she would see herself. This is the idealized image. She wanted to be young and thin. She wasn't. But she had identified herself so much with what she wanted that she was seeing herself just as she wanted.

The content of the idealized image

What the primary characteristic of this image will be depends on each person. To one it's strength. To another man – or, perhaps more often, to another woman – good looks. That is, one creates an idealized image of beauty. Another person creates for himself an idealized image of strength. Yet another has an idealized image of holiness. Do you know how many of us are saints today? A whole lot. We contemporary "good" Christians have more or less identified ourselves with an idealized image of holiness. That's why sometimes we rise up in arms so much over holiness. While we ourselves are a mess we rise up in arms, supposedly over holiness.

Others are influenced by an idealized image of honor. There are so many fathers and so many brothers who are touchy about the slightest stain on their daughter's or their sister's reputation. Certainly when a girl doesn't watch over her honor, this is in fact something bad for the girl herself and for her father and brothers. But if the brother comes to the point of killing his sister or the husband killing his wife or the father killing his daughter, or if they don't reach that point, in any case they become real tyrants toward the women in the family. This happens because they have identified themselves with an idealized image of honor.

How we can understand whether we have an idealized image inside us

The person who has an idealized image inside him and has identified in some way with it is arrogant, haughty. That is, he's acting completely out of character. We'll be able to understand whether we have an idealized image inside us and whether we're identified in some way with it from what we do when others don't acknowledge us for who we think we are. That is, the really holy person isn't disturbed at all, even if everyone condemns him, everyone spits on him, if you want me to put it like that. But just let someone turn up who challenges the holiness of that person who isn't really holy but thinks he is and has identified himself with an ideal image of holiness!

Certainly we don't mean by this that they're going to tell him to his face, "you're not a saint," and that this will disturb him. No. But when they behave toward him in such a way that they show him they don't take him seriously, that they don't pay much attention to him, then he'll be disturbed, he'll be uneasy, he'll get nervous and in any case he'll act in such a way that he'll show completely – both in his own eyes and in the eyes of others – that he doesn't have this legendary holiness he thinks he has.

Most often this is the reason that – allow me to say it – even we priests, the preachers, but also good Christians with offices, we rise up in arms, we get disturbed, perhaps we conduct a fearsome struggle and cause a big sensation about truth, about holiness. Basically we're not acting like this because at that moment we want to salvage truth and holiness in an objective way, but rather because we've identified ourselves with an idealized image of holiness, honor, virtue – and since others don't recognize it, we want to assert ourselves on them in this way.

The person who has something of some worth doesn't wait for others to recognize it. If they recognize it, good. And if they don't recognize it? Okay, so they don't recognize it. He doesn't get disturbed. It doesn't affect him at all. Have you seen a person who gets disturbed and trembles like a spring as soon as others don't recognize something in him? That person certainly doesn't have any of those things within him that he thinks he has, regardless of whether or not he has a reputation and whether he is known to be somebody.

As a rule the idealized image is unconscious

This idealized image is always, or rather for the most part, in the person's unconscious. One doesn't have an awareness that he's identified with an idealized image, that is, with a fantasy. And while all those around him realize that he isn't acting correctly, and while it's clear than he has a very inflated, very ostentatious and false idea about himself, he himself doesn't realize it.

He can sense in some way that he has a good opinion about himself, but in such a manner that the issue is entangled inside him. That's why, when he defends his idealized image, that is, his own imaginary virtue, he thinks he's defending objective virtue, objective holiness, high ideals and idealism. And so – forgive me for what I'm going to say – you see a person who is good for nothing from the viewpoint of real virtue, and he can make a big sensation about virtue, about holiness, about truth. Is he moved by a sincere motive? Is he moved by a pure motive? No way. Very simply that's the way he relaxes himself, that's the way he receives pleasure, that's the way his he vents, while he has this idealized image inside him, while he's identified with this imaginary picture, with the imaginary virtue he himself thinks he has. And he feels that if he defends virtue in the way he defends it, he's preserving his own virtue and his own holiness.

What people who are affected by the idealized image pay attention to

Of those who are affected by this illness, that is, those who have an idealized image about themselves, some pay attention to the idealized image in itself that they have, as they identify it with themselves. And you see, they can actually reach this point – they even consider their errors, their mistakes, and, I would say, even their sins – as the best things.

Others do have an idealized image of themselves, but they pay more attention to what they themselves are while remaining in the grip of their idealized image, that is, of what they want to be. They turn their interest towards their own reality. They are people who – not in a healthy way, if you please, but in an unhealthy way – are constantly dissatisfied for no reason at all.

The ascetic, the monk, beat themselves down like a fisherman will beat an octopus to soften it up, but they beat down their self in such a way that it's invigorated. The person, however, who wants to be his idealized image, who has an imaginary image about himself while in reality he's something else, pays attention to this "something else" that he is and criticizes himself, reprimands himself in an unhealthy way. He's literally displeased with himself for no reason at all. And of course he continually experiences a hellish condition inside him. He isn't invigorated, he isn't redeemed like the ascetic.

Another pays attention in an unhealthy way to both things, what he is and what he wants to be, and he starts out saying, "I should do this. I should do that. That other thing should happen." I know plenty of people who think that if they struggle a little bit more, they'll become saints. It's precisely these people who see what they are, they see also what they want to be, and they are stuck in this latter condition and move between the two. In this way they live continuously with a "should," and they are constantly accusing themselves of not having struggled yet. If only they struggled… What is this "if you struggled," my good man? Humble yourself, and let God have mercy on you.

All these things work in an unhealthy way. This means that the person who is gripped in this way by an idealized image is completely motionless with respect to forward progress. He doesn't move at all and he doesn't make spiritual progress. The idealized image is a barrier. It's something that stops the soul and doesn't let it develop. It's something that makes the person conceited, arrogant, haughty, egoistic. While the person who truly sees what he himself is and desires to reach a goal of some sort without being trapped by an idealized image, is humble and continually makes efforts placing his hope in God, having always the awareness of his sinfulness and his weakness. This person makes constant progress. On the contrary, the other is constantly stopped.

And please, in case we can't understand all the things I'm saying in any other way, let's look into them a little. How is our spiritual life going? Are we making progress or not? If we aren't making progress, if we determine that it's as if nothing is happening with us, surely something must exist inside us, which is as if it doesn't let us go one step further. And this, in any case, is an idealized image which has dwelled in our soul. That is, it's the very devil himself.

The Lord saw that all these things exist in man, and He came and became man Himself in order to tell us Who the true man is. The Lord Himself now sees these things in us who are baptized and reborn – potentially at least – and He wants very much to make us into true human beings. And He can do that as long as we decide to let go of all these idols our minds have created – because Christ came to crush the idols – and with a lot of humility, with a great deal of humility, run to Christ.

In these days we'll hear "Come, faithful, let us see where Christ was born."[1] That's where the lesson begins. Christ was born in a manger, in a cave. Christ was born humble. Only hidden in humility could God appear. Only when man humbles himself does God come and have mercy on him and make him one of His people.

I hope, my brothers, that this year, in these festive times, God will help us to become human beings to a little greater degree, in accordance with what we are saying here, and to have all those things we're talking about removed so that Christ may live in us.

---

1 First kathisma of the Orthros of Nativity.

The Idealized Image and Pride

Remember, before the feast days we had embarked on the great question of the idealized image, as it's called. And I think we should dwell on this question as much as we can and also concentrate as much of our attention on it as we can because we're all in the midst of this to a greater or lesser degree.

We were saying – so that we remember the question before we go any further – that every person, but especially the unhealthy type, has the tendency to create an imaginary image for himself. We would say that on account of the structure of our civilization and the whole spirit of our life contemporary man has a weakness for this illness. In particular the unhealthy person has the tendency to want to be something, and that's why he creates for himself an idealized image, that is, an imaginary image about himself, which is something extremely lofty, and somehow he identifies with it. That is, he himself is something else, but he thinks that his very self is this image – which certainly most often is subconscious. He doesn't understand that he has created something of this sort. But all the same this image is operating, and it does its work from the subconscious.

Far from reality

Before the feast days when we first took up the question, we were saying that this image is flattering for him who creates it. And allow me to refer again to the sketch that had been published in a newspaper. A woman who was old and not well-proportioned, that is, chubby, was looking into a mirror. And in the mirror the cartoonist was presenting the lady as young and thin, that is, as she would like herself to be. She herself was reflected in the mirror, but paradoxically she herself was presented in it as she would like to be and as she almost thought and believed she was.

We would say that the idealized image is something of the sort. When you look into the mirror, you'll see yourself as you are. Photographers improve on us. That is, although they photograph us, they also manage to improve on us. The mirror, however, shows us just as we are. So then, while the image we have of ourselves should be what we really are, one who has been influenced by this illness – if you want us to call the idealized image in this way – doesn't manage to see himself as he is, but sees himself in his idealized image. And he certainly sees himself in a completely different way. And of course the idealized image is commensurate with the greatest weakness someone has. One person has a weakness in regard to good looks, another has a weakness in regard to something else.

The idealized image is something unreal, something imaginary. Our self, however, is something real. So the further away this image is from reality, from what we are, the prouder the person is, the more high-minded and arrogant the person is. With the fall what happened to man? This sort of thing happened – man doesn't know exactly what he is, he relies on something else, and each person creates an image for himself. And the further away this image is from reality, the greater the pride, the egoism, the arrogance. And we were saying that in practice it appears like this – the further away this image is from reality, the more someone is ready to get angry as soon as people happen to make a remark of some sort, as soon as people happen to say something that belittles him, something that isn't contained in the image he has of himself.

As long as a little shack stands firmly on its foundations, it doesn't need anyone to prop it up so that it doesn't collapse.

Only the shack that is ready to collapse needs support. So when a person really has virtue, when he really is something, he doesn't fear that he might happen to collapse. That is, he doesn't fear that he will happen to lose something of what he is, when one person has told him this and someone else has told him something else.

When someone is frightened, very uneasy, gets excited, flares up, has an outburst as soon as people tell him something (which of course isn't something good), this means that he's in the grip of an idealized image. He doesn't know his real self. And precisely because this idealized image isn't something that stands firmly, that is firmly established so that in this way there is no danger of its collapsing, but is simply an image, that's why it's in danger of collapsing when one person strikes it here and another strikes it there. And someone hurries to prop it up with his anger, with his outburst, with his assault, with his vindictiveness. He gives himself away, certainly, he becomes ridiculous, and everybody understands what's happening except the person himself. As we've explained, precisely because this whole situation is extremely unconscious, that's why it's possible for everyone else to understand what we are while we don't understand. This is the reason that we sometimes see a person speaking in such a way – for example, praising himself – where someone says, "But what's he saying now? It he in his right mind?" Because what he's saying is completely out of touch with reality. He, however, thinks he's in his right mind. He doesn't understand that what he's saying is completely out of touch with reality. He doesn't understand that there's something else inside him that makes him express himself and behave like that. He doesn't understand, although others understand.

Could it be that I'm out of touch with reality?

Before we move on, let's say this. Let's not be surprised when we see people behave in a senseless way. Let's not be surprised. It's very simply that, these people find themselves in a situation that is very far from reality, and it's necessary for us to help them as best as we can to come back down to reality.

On the other hand, when we see others get somewhat surprised at our own behavior and sometimes misunderstand us, let's ask ourselves: "Why are the others surprised? Why do they misunderstand us? What's happening? Could it be that we're out of touch with reality, in the grip of an idealized image, and everyone else recognizes it while we don't?" That is, while all the others see what we are, we don't see it and that's why we admire ourselves. And of course, on top of everything else, one becomes ridiculous besides.

It's not just poorly educated people who suffer from this, but also the educated. You see that the other person is very wise since he has learned many things, but with respect to this question he's sick. How many times do we see people bragging? We feel like saying to them, "My good man, you're so exalted. Everybody sees this, they honor you, they respect you. Do you need to express yourself like this?" But he doesn't understand. Why? Because there's a great distance between his reality and the idealized image he has inside himself about himself.

The Disorganization of the Person

He sees his shortcomings as virtues

Our topic is the idealized image. The idealized image – we said – is a figment of the person's imagination. It's something non-existent, but he believes in it as something existent. A person creates this image – which dwells inside him – and it applies more influence over its creator in proportion to where the center of gravity of his interest falls.

In our previous talk we emphasized that a person creates the idealized image for the most part subconsciously. And while it's expressed in daily life and other people see it and make fun of us, we don't realize it precisely because it's subconscious. That's why, as we were saying, we shouldn't be surprised when we see a person do thoughtless things, do nonsensical things – swagger about, boast about himself up to the point of making a fool of himself – without realizing it. We mustn't be surprised because he's influenced by the idealized image found in his subconscious.

One who has created such an idealized image, as he identifies himself with it, thinks of himself as a man who is distinguished from others, like a great genius. He sees even his shortcomings as good and holy, as virtues. And we shouldn't be surprised when someone has perpetrated a frightful mistake, an error, more concretely he has committed a sin, and he keeps trying to persuade us, too, that this wasn't by any means an error or the manifestation of a shortcoming, but it was a manifestation of virtue. Let's not be surprised because in all probability, this person is influenced by an idealized image and in fact he's identified with it.

Unhealthy self-criticism

Another person, who also has an idealized image about himself, may not concentrate so much of his attention on it. On the one hand he sees it, but he concentrates his attention and his interest on his own situation. Be careful, now. He sees himself, he sees his own reality in relation to the idealized image, to this perfect image he has in his imagination, and as he compares them, he wants his own reality to be this perfect image. But of course it isn't and it can't be. And this very comparison causes him to create, in some way, an image for himself which is lower, more lowly, than his own reality, and then he begins this severe self-criticism. He begins to quarrel with himself, to worry himself sick, as they say, for no reason at all. He doesn't do this in a constructive manner, as the Fathers teach us, as the Gospel says, as true humility prescribes, but in an unhealthy way.

From what I have understood personally, a great many Christians suffer from this today, who are influenced by the idealized image that they have created within their mind about themselves. But since their self is not in reality this idealized image that they have created but something else, this causes them – as they make the comparison – to see themselves as much lower than they are. And that's where despondency, grievance, grumbling begin. These people begin to complain, as we say, for no reason at all.

Of course rather than progress, on the contrary we have depression, morbidity – in the bad sense – disaster, a collapse and not an ascent. While true humility, true repentance, compunction and self-criticism – as the Fathers live it and teach it – raise a person up.

"Should…"

In other people a third thing happens. They see the idealized image, they also see themselves, but neither to the one nor to the other do they pay so much attention as they pay attention to the distance that exists between the two images. And of course, they want to eliminate this distance, to minimize it. They want to make it go away if possible, for this distance to be completely wiped out, so that it doesn't exist. That is, in the final analysis they want the one image, that is, the reality of themselves, to be identical to the idealized image. And you see these people, those, that is, who are influenced somewhat in this way by the idealized image, continually finding themselves with the word "should" – "I should do this, I should do that."

With my own eyes I've seen it happen this way to many souls. They are those people, as we were also saying before the feast days,[1] if you recall, who believe that they would definitely have achieved their idealized image, they would have been their perfect images, perfect people, if they had struggled – but they haven't struggled yet! This is supposedly the whole issue! If they struggle, if they make the effort, they'll arrive at the perfect image they have in their imagination. And that's why, I repeat, they live with this "should," but with such a disposition that they never take a single step forward. This is a proof that they don't even see themselves correctly, and this image isn't real, but it's an imaginary image that they created inside their minds, and in an extremely egoistic way they want to reach it, and that's why this inactivity, this immobility is created inside them.

That is, this person who is influenced by the idealized image – by this imaginary image that he has about himself,

---

1 See the talk "Identifying with a fantasy" p. 115 ff.

that he wants to have about himself or at which he wants his own self to arrive – is completely powerless, completely sluggish, completely static. He finds himself in a static condition and he can't even take a single step forward. While the person who has humility within him, who is inspired by the humility of the Gospel, by the humility the Fathers teach, makes continual progress. And he doesn't live with anguish, which is always present in the one who is influenced by the idealized image.

The idealized image is a substitute for self-confidence

In order for us to make a little progress, let me say here that the idealized image is often a substitute for self-confidence. That is – as I understand it – this imaginary image, which is of course egoism through and through – about this there is absolutely no doubt – comes in a certain way into the person's soul and devours the person, disintegrates him, dissolves him to such a point that there's no vitality within him, there's no capability, will, there's no sentimentalism, no movement, no disposition and desire for effort, for struggle. And this happens because the idealized image utterly consumes and takes the place of the person's self-confidence – in the good sense of the word self-confidence.

The person must rely on God. However, as God created him in His image, the human being is something of value. And with this something the person will make progress, relying on God, on God's grace, having trust in God. If this something is dissolved, disorganized, where we see the splitting of personality created inside a person that appears in many people today, after that the person can't even do anything nor can he make progress, and it isn't even possible for him to rely on God, on God's grace.

This is what we've said other times as well in relation to the trust that we ought to have in God. When I stretch out my hand and ask someone for a glass of water, and my hand trembles, a reasonable person will not possibly place a glass full of water into this hand. How is he going to place it there? The water will spill immediately.

In a soul that is disorganized, destroyed, in a soul in which this image has been dissolved from the way God formed it – that is, in the image of God – and the soul has been divided, has experienced the division that we're talking about, God can't give His help, His strengthening, His power, His grace. From this viewpoint, then, there's need for a kind of self-confidence. That is, there's need for the feeling that we exist, the feeling that we were created in the image and according to the likeness of God, and that we're receptive of God's offering. The idealized image, however, comes along and dissolves all that. It casts all that out of our existence. As I said, it disorganizes and deadens man's inner world, that is, it renders it useless.

Something of the sort happens in those souls which often discover something analogous in themselves and perhaps come to their spiritual father and say, "I have no interest in anything, I can't struggle. I feel a deadness, an inaction, a tepidity." That is, an unhealthy situation has been created in this soul, and certainly to a somewhat advanced degree. Here the apostle Paul would say, "Awake, O sleeper and arise from the dead, and Christ shall give you light."[2] Let go of the idealized images and repent sincerely before God. Really humble yourself sincerely before God and look at this little thing that you are. Rely on this little thing – support your

---
2 Ephesians 5:14.

hand, we would say, and don't let it tremble – and ask your heavenly Father to give you His help. And He'll give it to you.

And God knows how far He will lead you and what will happen. It's not for you to say where you will arrive, up to what point you'll progress, and what will happen. Your task is for you to find your means, for you to see where you are, to stand there and to hope boundlessly and absolutely in Almighty God.

Unfavorable Influences of Contemporary Society

Competition: the shackles of today's man

The weakest, the most sinful, the most narrow-minded person, one who doesn't understand much or know much, when he decides to let himself go to God's grace, he'll be redeemed.

We must emphasize next something that may have escaped our notice. We usually say, "Here in the midst of the world, in the midst of society, among other people, it's worthwhile for someone to struggle, to be able to cope and to help others. Here is where a person is tested. Here is where it will be shown if one is in fact faithful and if in the end one will be saved."

This is certainly a true statement. But the way things are, especially in our days, in our times – let's not go back to previous years – as a person lives in society, among other people, he finds himself in a continuous competition. Each of us is constantly judging himself and comparing himself with others. So he can't easily and freely accept that he is what he is and let himself go to God easily, freely, humbly and with a sense of his reality. The result is that he becomes entangled. And, I repeat, while someone is a man of God, a man of the Church, of the Gospel, a good person who wants to do something as a Christian, in spite of all this he gets mixed up. He gets caught up in this whirlpool, in these chains and shackles that contemporary society creates, and he remains there. Yes, on the one hand a person recognizes and acknowledges that sin exists, but still he constantly whirls around it, he's continuously occupied with it, he continuously pays attention to it, resulting in the creation of complexes inside the person, complications, an idealized image, and other abnormal conditions, as we've said.

The person, however, who will escape from this whole snare that exists in society and will no longer have the worry of comparing himself to others and competing against them in order that he too can stand before them and among them, but who will have as his sole concern to find himself alone with God alone, will be – as a rule, certainly – redeemed from such unnatural psychological conditions.

For example, from what we know, it's inconceivable for one who is going to decide to become a monastic – I'm not saying that someone should do this, but let's recognize the truth – that is, he'll go to the Holy Mountain or somewhere else to become a monastic, it's inconceivable, that is, it's something that will not enter people's minds about such a person, that there he'll compare himself with others, he'll compete with them and think about how he can surpass others, how he can become superior to them. That is, how he'll be able in this way to confirm his existence among others. And for that reason – certainly as long as there is a good attitude, as long as he knows why he went there – in the end he manages with God's help and with the help of some man of the Church to be released to the love of God, to accept the love and the offering of God and be saved.

Salvation is extremely simple. It isn't as complicated as we sometimes imagine, nor so difficult as we sometimes think. Salvation is very simple because it's offered to man freely by God. It's offered by God to a person for whom God knows in advance that he's completely unworthy of this salvation, but He gives it to him for free.

How the idealized image is created

So, then, when someone lives in this society, he gets entangled in competition, in this comparison, he can't stand naked before God, he can't stand humbly, simply before God with nothing but the readiness to accept God's offering and love. He makes an effort to stand among others, as we said, to compete against them. But how will he be able to stand, since each of us – whether we understand it or not, even that one who looks to be the strongest – each of us deep inside has a sense, subconscious perhaps, of his weakness?

There is no person who at the depth of his existence doesn't sense his weakness even a little, since this weakness continually and constantly accompanies him. But on the other hand he's continually and constantly compelled by his affairs to project an effort to confirm his existence among others and to be able to stand, himself too, among others, just as he compares himself with others and competes with them. This means that he should have something within him that will support him.

If I may, let me offer an example. Suppose many of us are gathered in some vast space, thousands of people, and in one spot someone is speaking to all of us, and we want to see him. It's utterly impossible for us to see him unless he is situated higher than us. Therefore for a person to be able to see, a platform of some sort needs to be placed under his feet to help him rise up.

So, then, in order for a person to stand among people and feel comfortable, to feel secure, he wants to sense himself higher, he wants to sense that he's above others. And in order to accomplish this, he sets his foot somewhere, he leans against something. That is, he puts something into his existence, something which is of course fake, fabricated, and supporting himself on it, stepping on it, he escapes from reality.

At the moment, for example, that a person has a tendency toward great holiness, or another person has a tendency toward great harshness, at that moment, however strange it appears, he has within him this something on which he wants to stand. At the moment that someone has within him a tendency toward great love or a tendency toward absolute indifference toward others, he puts something fake inside him, something on which he wants to support himself, to step on, in order to appear above others.

You must know that when something about a person is very striking – it's being discussed a lot, it's projected a lot, it's unusual – this isn't real, it isn't normal. It's something that's out of touch with reality. It's an expression of the idealized image that exists in that person.

We may see a person chase after holiness, and deep inside this person doesn't have any connection to holiness. Or it's possible for us to see a person chase after love and talk constantly about love and go to great trouble about it, and deep inside he doesn't have a trace of love. All these things are phony, and he does them precisely in order to be able to step onto something, to support himself somewhere, so as to feel above others, to feel loftier than others.

Let's keep it in mind, then, that as things are today, contemporary society in which we live doesn't offer itself at all for a person to be with his real self and to have the courage and the guts to stand before God with this real self, to have recourse to God and to seek from God His love, His grace, His salvation that He offers. The reality of contemporary society is such that it entangles a person in the gears of sin.

In itself sin is a bad thing, but there exists the love of God, there exists the salvation God offers. But things are such today that contemporary society, the spirit of contemporary society entangles even the good Christian in the gears of sin, and one is altered. That is, he believes that he's something other than what he is, and in the end he becomes incapable of receiving God's grace. Certainly none of these things mean that someone should run away from society. Because perhaps many of us, even if we want to run away, we can't.

Let's ask ourselves

All these things tell us that we must have in mind this great danger, we must pay attention constantly and ask ourselves: Is it possible that it happens, even at the moment we believe in God, even at the moment that we are religious people and partake of the mysteries of the Church, and the moment that we are touchy about any blemish against Christ's truth and we do this or that, is it possible that we happen to find ourselves in delusion? Is it possible that at the moment we happen to express ourselves this way or that, we're victims of an image that each of us has created inside him about himself? Is it possible that we happen to be out of touch with reality and that we're living in the land of fantasy? And there is no hope to arrive at truth by means of fantasy, by means of those phony things.

Truth comes by itself to man. It's not found by man. Salvation comes by itself to man. It's not found by man. Sanctification come by itself to man. God gives it. It's not found by man. These things come, however, when man doesn't want to create his own holiness, his own salvation, or I don't know what else, but he remains there where he is and opens himself completely to what God offers. True asceticism, the true struggle and the true effort on man's part, is not that man will do something, but for man to be able to open his existence so that God can put what He wants into it.

The Idealized Image Replaces Ideals

The idealized image and the journey toward Christ

Among other things, we said in the previous gathering[1] that the idealized image which each person shapes in himself substitutes for self-confidence. In this talk we're going to refer to the fact that the idealized image also substitutes for the person's ideals.

Precisely because man doesn't come from himself, isn't self-existent, but comes from somewhere else and depends on something else, in some way he seeks something outside himself that will support him. Man can't be supported only on himself. We could say, then, that ideals play such a role.

You must have heard people say – or perhaps even you yourselves have found yourselves in a position of saying – "My life doesn't have any meaning." The person who says that his life doesn't have any meaning has no ideals. Beyond the fact that someone who says such a thing can't be a person of faith and it's impossible to say that he truly believes in God, he also doesn't have any ideals. He can't have ideals.

In the person who is going to create an idealized image, the idealized image comes into his existence precisely in that place where his ideals should be. If you like, let's say more concretely that if I'm ruled by an idealized image I've created, it isn't possible for me truly to believe in Christ, to turn towards Christ, to journey towards Christ, to depend on Christ. It's impossible. Because what would cause me to be brought to Christ is already engaged and ruled by the idealized image and so there's no room for Christ.

---

[1] See the talk "The Disintegration of the Person" pp. 126 ff.

You may have noticed that many people – especially in our days – as they struggle, they try, they rush to accomplish something, when they end up not succeeding in what they strive for, what they exert themselves for and what they seek, but they have a complete failure, they feel as if they're destroyed, as if they're lost and they can't bear life. This is what I said earlier, that life no longer has any meaning for them.

This means two things. First, how much harm the idealized image causes us. Because if we create an idealized image and we're in the grip of it and we fill our soul with it, our soul can't turn in any other direction. And the second thing is that precisely because we feel that we're destroyed if we lose this idealized image, we don't allow it in any way to escape from us, nor do we dare to admit that it's mistaken, that it's a lie, a mirage. Because as soon as we believe that it's a lie, a mirage, something nonexistent, we feel that we're destroyed.

And here lies the great difficulty encountered by the specialist who occupies himself with circumstances of this sort. That is, when he has to do with such a person, it's extremely difficult to get him to understand that he should detach himself from this idealized image and look in another direction and desire something else, pursue something else. Such a person is not able to understand, precisely because – by the mere thought of it – disaster lurks within his existence since, as we said, his existence is supported on the idealized image. It's another matter now that on the other hand the idealized image is tearing apart his inner world.

The idealized image goes away very slowly

We should also keep in mind that this idealized image will go away from within us very slowly. It's very difficult for it to go away suddenly. The person has to have a lot of faith in order for this idealized image to go away quickly. It will go away from us very slowly. This should be taken into account by both the person who is trying to help such a person, but by also the one who is going to be helped. Because if we try to remove this idealized image immediately, we'll do harm instead of good.

I'll mention an example from the *Gerontikon*. One of the abbas says, "If you see someone doing some spiritual deed, and you understand that he's doing it completely out of egoism, don't stop him."[2] Another abba, however, says, "If you see someone ascending to heaven by his own will, grab him by the foot and pull him down."[3]

In any case, in the saying we're quoting here, the abba says, "If you see someone doing some spiritual deed out of

---

[2] See *The World of the Desert Fathers: Stories and Sayings from the Anonymous Series of the Apophthegmata Patrum*. tr. with introduction by Columba Stewart, OSB, Kalamazoo, MI – Spencer, MA: Cistercian Publications, 1986. XL (111) p. 37 "The old men used to say, 'If you see a young man climbing toward heaven by his own will, grab his foot and pull him down, for it will be for his own good."

[3] Greek text of this exchange between two of the Fathers can be found in *To Mega Gerontikon*, published by the Holy Monastery of The Nativity of the Theotokos, vol. 3. Panorama Thessaloniki 1997. Chapter I, § 271. It has not been possible so far to locate this *apophthegma* in an English-language edition. For the reader's convenience, therefore, the passage is translated below from the *Mega Gerontikon*: One of the Fathers said: "I hate to see young monks engage in vainglory; they labor and gain no reward because they aim at the glory of men."

Another Elder, who had a better grasp of things, said to him, "I accept them with great pleasure. It is better for a young man to be vainglorious than to be negligent, because when he aims at vainglory, he necessarily becomes self-controlled and keeps vigil and exposes himself to cold and acquires love and undergoes difficulties to gain praise. After such a way of life, God's grace visits him and speaks to him as follows: 'Why are you working not for Me but for men?' Then he is persuaded not to have his attention turned toward human glory but toward the glory of God." "Indeed" – said the other Elder when he heard this – "That is the way things are." [translator's note] egoism, don't stop him. Let him do it." For the abba to say this, he knew something of what we're saying about the idealized image. What is the meaning of his words? That he's certainly doing this spiritual deed out of egoism, and yet he's doing something and not remaining inactive. Well, one of these days he'll understand that his whole work is wasted since he does it out of egoism, and he may repent and start to do his work with humility. If you hinder him, though, you'll cause him to be completely deadened, overtaken by inaction, by laziness, by sloth, by lack of interest in spiritual things. We would say he will be overtaken by disappointment, by hopelessness, by a feeling that he doesn't have any purpose in life, that his life doesn't have any meaning and he could go straight ahead and kill himself.

This, then, is the meaning here of the idealized image. It plays this role in this circumstance – it replaces a person's ideals, it replaces the person's genuine inclinations for this or that. And as it replaces all those things, the person remains without ideals, he remains simply with the idealized image, which in the end even leads him by the nose.

Let me mention an example so that we're not at a loss about what sometimes happens to us. We believe in Christ, in the Church, in the Gospel. We pursue, we seek holiness, prayer, all those good things. But while you try to do something good, you see you're doing something else. Because your ideal – Christ, the Church, or holiness – no longer has any power to guide you, to govern your existence. And although you see this, you can't do anything because in reality you find yourself somewhere else, you are dwelling somewhere else. You see the ideals on the one hand, but they're outside your existence. Inside you, in the place where the ideals should be, is the idealized image. That is, something else has been ruling over you.

How inflexible the idealized image is

As we proceed now we should make a little effort to see how inflexible this idealized image is. Inflexible. It isn't affected by words or by anything else. It doesn't budge an inch from inside us. It's established there, it holds us captive, but we also hold it captive. And it holds onto us, but we hold onto it also. Because if we stop holding onto it, it will go away. What is it going to do?

The idealized image works from inside there in a defensive way. Let's imagine an impregnable fort. Nothing can sack it, nothing can approach it. In exactly this way the idealized image is established inside us. And we see everything by means of this image. It causes us to see things as we see them.

Suppose we have an old wall. If we make a painting on this old wall, the wall won't appear old. In this way the person can be full of passions, weaknesses, he can have mistakes, errors, but he doesn't see them precisely because he puts this idealized image on top of them.

Shall we go still further? One person sees things this way because he has this type of idealized image. Another person sees things differently because he has another type of idealized image. More concretely. In one person who is a compliant type, who moves toward people, as we've said – in a person, that is, who needs others, who depends on others, who is attached to others – his idealized image is created in accord with his psychology, in accord with this psychological make-up of his. And so whatever serves this tendency he has is for him a virtue. Only what is contrary to this tendency does he see as a sin, as wickedness. That is, the fear someone has inside him, the cowardice he has, a tendency he has to be attached, he doesn't by any means see these things as sins, as shortcomings, so as to strike them down mercilessly. On the contrary, an aggressive type – the type who moves against people – sees things such as fear, cowardice, a disposition to show understanding toward others, a disposition for adjustment, and so forth – as the greatest sins. As on the other hand he sees as virtues attacking everyone continually, criticizing, knocking down continually and examining others.

The collective idealized image

Here let me say that in the various organized religious groups that exist, perhaps an idealized image is created, without their realizing it, in keeping with the psychology each group has, with the psychological make-up its members have, and from that point on you realize what happens. That's why we don't communicate with one another.

One organized group over here, one organized group over there, yet another organized group over yonder. It doesn't matter that each group has its program, has its task, has this or that expressions. What matters is that each one in his group creates his own ethics. In a certain way each one in his group creates his own Gospel, or, rather, we would say, he interprets the Gospel in his own way and creates his own ethics. And so something that is seen as a virtue in this group can be seen as a vice in the other group. And something that is seen as a virtue there, here can be seen as a vice.

We should be very careful of these things. That is, it's possible today, in our days, that we Christians are victims in one way or another. The Fathers would say it straightforwardly – victims of our egoism, of our arrogance, victims of our love of ourselves, of our self-love.

Let me say this in conclusion. This idealized image which plagues me can be an idealized image I created all by myself. But it can also be an idealized image that we've all created together. That is, since we agree, since we all have the same psychology, and it is this one thing, this fake thing, the devil has managed to create this idealized image, and that is what leads us hither and yon. And in this way we don't see Christ nor do we live Christ; nor do we get to know the true Gospel, and as a consequence we are not able to understand it and live it and apply it correctly.

The Idealized Image: Our Imaginary Self

The fictitious image and elements of reality

The idealized image – the topic that has been occupying us in our most recent gatherings – can be characterized as our fictitious or imaginary self. That is, it's something that doesn't exist in reality, but rather we've created it, we've fashioned it, we've imagined it ourselves. The bad thing is – perhaps it can also be good, who knows where there is more truth, but let's take it that way – the bad thing is that most often there are elements of reality entangled with this imaginary and fictitious image.

Let's explain. Someone truly believes in God, he wants to believe in God. He truly believes in the Church, he wants to believe in the Church. He truly wants to live the Christian life. These are real elements. They are a necessity of his soul, they are operations of his soul. On the other hand, however, this person – either because he isn't very sincere before God and before himself and others, or because he's a psychologically unhealthy type – creates an idealized image and he binds himself to it. And so in the end this idealized, imaginary, fictitious image is tangled up with real elements. Then a labyrinth is created in this way and one can't make heads or tails of it.

Now we're discussing these things here, we talk every so often and speak more concretely about the idealized image. I wonder how many of you may have asked yourselves – and from what I know from confidential conversations and confession, a fair number of you should have asked yourselves – "Is it possible that I, too, have an idealized image?" On the other hand someone sees himself and questions himself – "Since I truly accept the Gospel, I truly believe, I truly struggle, I truly want to be a Christian, where, after all, is this idealized image?"

Here the matter gets even more tangled up since the imaginary and the fictitious elements are entangled with the real elements. All the same, however, the idealized image – this imaginary thing, this fictitious thing, which is our imaginary and fictitious self – always prevails over our real self and substitutes for it. That is, the unhealthy type considers the imaginary, the idealized image as real and identifies with it, and this fictitious, idealized image ends up overshadowing the real person, our real self. From that point on all the problems finally begin. And while one struggles and tries to be a Christian, he ends up being neither a Christian nor faithful and he has neither virtue nor a spiritual life, and wonders what's going on.

Moving ahead a little more, let's say that the idealized image ensures an equilibrium in the person who has it. Many people would literally fall to pieces, would go crazy, would completely lose themselves if this idealized image were not there to save them. That is, up to a certain point it does something good, but it's a fictitious thing – how else can we deal with it? – and it can't last forever. One of these days the bomb is going to go off.

Repression of the idealized image

Next I'd like to refer to something else. Often someone represses this idealized image he has and which he identifies with. This is even worse. In this case one ceases to be identified with his idealized image anymore and to be concentrated on it and given to it, and since it's repressed, he transfers it to another person. This means that from that point on he ceases to have a good opinion of himself, and instead he begins to admire someone else.

So many times – we Christians suffer from this more often – one admires someone, but he doesn't admire the person himself, he doesn't even see the person himself, but he simply transfers to him the idealized image he has inside him. And when one admires this person, when one loves this person, when he wears himself out serving this person, when he subjects himself to this person and is even ready to throw himself into a fire for this person's benefit, he does nothing else but love, idolize and fawn upon his own idealized image, which he didn't have the courage to see in himself and instead he has transferred it to another person.

This is the reason that some souls are literally disappointed when the facts demonstrate that the person they had relied on so much, whom they had idolized so much, they had admired so much, isn't at all like what they were thinking. Unfortunately, in recent years quite a few such things have happened and we're still having a rough time trying to support these souls. And so this soul literally collapses, disappointed, as if God, Christ did not exist, as if the Church, the Gospel did not exist. Because for this soul the Gospel, the Church, Christ, were this person who was like a god inside this soul. And, as I said, this soul is disappointed, it collapses, unless it can be supported either with someone's help or by itself in order, in the end, to remain faithful to God and be able in this way to find God, and there to give all its being and there to find its true, real ideal. And after it humbles itself before God, to be able to have a personal relation directly with God and not by means of other persons.

Are We Serving an Idol?

Setting aside our real self

In relation to the idealized image we've said that it's our imaginary, fictitious self, but at the same time it also has real elements.

Let me speak one more time about something that happens with a certain number of Christians. One believes in God, believes in the Gospel, believes in Christianity, believes in the Church. This faith is a real quest on the part of his soul. But since the soul doesn't move correctly – and this happens since conflicts are created within it because it doesn't take within it the correct position before God, before itself, and before others – it seeks on the one hand, but in the end what it seeks, what it looks for, isn't what it really should seek and look for, but something the soul fashions by itself. In other words, it's an idealized image.

For example, the soul seeks its holiness, it seeks perfection. "You must be perfect," says the Lord Himself, "as your heavenly Father is perfect."[1] "Strive… for holiness,"[2] says the Apostle Paul.

The bad thing isn't that he aims at holiness, that he aims at perfection. But while holiness is a real search and an inclination of the soul, when the person doesn't seek it correctly, then he fashions an idealized image – that is, a fake, fictitious, imaginary image of holiness, of perfection – and identifies it with himself.

And in the final analysis, since all the inclinations and searchings of the soul, since all the operations and expressions of the soul are directed toward this

---

1 Matthew 5: 48.
2 Hebrews 12:14.

idealized image, the personality is set aside, our most important self is set aside. Our real self is set aside, it goes off into a corner and what remains is this fictitious thing, this imaginary thing. We, however, think that we really strive for holiness, perfection – that which we should be seeking and striving for – and that it is this that we work for, it is this that we tire ourselves for, this that we serve. In the final analysis, however, we're serving and worshipping something imaginary, something chimerical, something that – if you want me to put it this way now – is an idol.

Certainly none of these things are accidental and they don't happen all by themselves. Something is at fault in the person's roots. Perhaps these disturbances and these conflicts have existed from childhood years, perhaps from teenage years. And since the soul can't bear to live with these conflicts, with this disorder that exists within it, but at the same time it can't provide a correct solution, it takes refuge in the idealized image.

Why does the person bind himself so closely to the idealized image?

The idealized image is actually good for us up to a certain point, as we were saying last time. That is, a great many people – and we don't mean only other people, but especially Christians, good Christians – a great many good Christians, then, who are attached to this idealized image precisely because they are bound to it, manage to appear balanced, calm, superior, and in this way they have demands and claims on others in life.

But as soon as something, an incident, some event, undermines this idealized image – since it's imaginary, fictitious and not real – one is compelled to see his real self. If someone steps on a board which isn't well supported, even if he who steps on it thinks that it's supported wonderfully, as soon as someone pulls this board away, he'll fall down. And so when this image is undermined, one is compelled to see his real self – to see his nakedness, his shortcomings, to see the conflicts and all the confusion that exists inside him.

From what the specialists say, but also from what we ourselves are able to comprehend by means of the facts, it is something very important for the person to see – after an event, after a shocking occurrence – that he isn't who he thought he was, and to see himself in such a way that he can no longer stand to live; to feel that he's falling, that he's lost, that he's crushed.

And so it's a good thing for a person to find himself in such a situation. It's an opportunity for him to stop living with his imaginary, fictitious self, to make a decision to come down to earth and begin his life from the beginning. And from that point on to live with his real self; to see his real self and to move with it toward God, to seek God, to seek holiness, perfection. But it's very difficult for this to happen; very difficult.

As we were saying another time – imagine that we're in an airplane and at a certain moment they tell us, "Jump from the airplane." And one was to jump into the void. A parachutist is taught slowly, gradually, and finally he learns to jump. But to someone who doesn't know and they simply give him a parachute and tell him, "Jump," it's very difficult. Even someone who has decided to kill himself may not do it. He'd be especially afraid when things compel him, in a way, to jump from the airplane. It's that difficult.

As difficult as it is, then, for someone to jump from an airplane into the void, it's equally difficult and even more difficult for him to let himself go into this void that's created in his existence as his idealized image departs from inside him. That's why, then, the person is very tightly bound to this idealized image and in some way he doesn't want to let go of it.

Even to death for the idealized image

And we've said on a previous occasion – and we should say it, and say it again and repeat it – that we shouldn't be at all surprised when we see a person being, as we say, hard-headed and not being able to understand something, not being able to change his opinion about something.

Shall I say something else now? Do you think it'll be too much? I don't imagine it's too much. Someone can go all the way to death when it's a question of saving his idealized image. That's why some people reach the point of suicide. They may even throw themselves into a fire, as the expression goes. That is, it won't be so difficult for this person to throw himself into a fire and be burnt, because at least in this way he departs with the conviction that he's something. He departs with this superiority, this perfection of his. He departs being identified with the idealized image he has.

Whether one likes it or not, however, at some point the facts force him to abandon his idealized image. At that point some people finally find their real self. Some manage to return to the idealized image, while others suffer psychologically, and God knows what will become of them.

The person who is bound up in this way with the idealized image is as if he has a building, a house – if you want me to put it like that – that he feels is supported very well, that it's built on a good foundation, and yet this house is full of dynamite which can blow up at any moment and blast the house into the air. That's why such a person, peaceful, calm, humble, important – not only in his own eyes, but unfortunately others sometimes see him that way too – doesn't accept objections, doesn't accept criticisms, doesn't agree to change his mind.

This is the person who can't bear it when people don't recognize him, he can't stand it when people don't admire him. He's the person who avoids life and its pitfalls. He tries not to let people see that he's a regular person like other people. He always tries to do what he's sure he can do and where there's no chance for him to fail. He can't stand to lay himself open to criticism, to appear to have fallen into error, to appear to be like everybody else. What relaxes him, what supports him is to for him to think and for others to think that he stands extremely high.

This person, then, can't live without people's admiration, without their flattery. He is very dependent on others, very much bound up with others, despite the fact that he appears to be isolated.

Projection of the idealized image and its consequences

And allow me to say yet one more time that to such a person something even worse can happen – that he can repress this idealized image with which he's identified. That is, he doesn't seek in himself nor does he see in himself the holiness, the perfection – certainly that's what he thinks, but in reality it doesn't happen that way – but he has repressed it, he has pushed deep within himself the idealized image about holiness and he doesn't even reflect on it at all. He projects it, however, from deep down where it is, onto someone else. We Christians suffer a great deal from this. In particular you spiritual children suffer from this a great deal with us priests, who are supposed to be spiritual fathers. That is, it could be that one of you can't stand to consider himself to be identified with an image of holiness, with an image of perfection, but at the same time he has that inside him and since he can't live otherwise, in the end he sees it in someone else.

Let's say a certain spiritual son, as we usually put it, knows a spiritual father and something about this spiritual father makes an impression on the spiritual son. Afterwards, the fictitious, the imaginary image he has about holiness and about perfection, this idealized image that this spiritual son has inside himself which he can't live without, he projects it onto the spiritual father. And as a consequence he doesn't see him as he is but as his idealized image has fashioned him inside himself.

And so the attachment to the spiritual father manifests itself, the admiration begins, he begins to see even the spiritual father's shortcomings as virtues and as great accomplishments, he begins to see this, he begins to see that. And as you realize, there can be a lot of ugly consequences. And when in fact the spiritual father – or anyone else on whom he has projected his idealized image and to whom he has attached himself – happens to appear to be a regular person and not a saint and perfect person as this spiritual son thinks, then this spiritual son, who had relied on him so much, is devastated and falls apart. That is – so that we understand better – it's as if God were lost, as if God were destroyed. That's how much the person suffers. These things aren't strange or odd. They are things that happen among us, and we should pay a lot of attention.

Let's love God, let's believe in God, let's seek God truly, correctly. And as soon as we see that a person – either ourselves or someone else – takes God's place in our existence, we should know that a great evil has found us, and by every sacrifice and in every way we must look to cast them out of our hearts – even our self, as I said, our false self, this idealized image – and to have God remain there alone.

We find ourselves in danger if we don't pay attention

If, then, all these things we're saying are true – and allow me to say that perhaps I know something about these things and I believe that they are more or less true – you understand the danger we find ourselves in if we don't pay attention.

More generally the life we're living as people in this world, but especially the Christian life, isn't fun and games. God is great, and He's ready to help man; there's no room for any doubt. Salvation is given for free and it's extremely easy. But from this aspect, however, the person gets things mixed up and seeks salvation elsewhere, since deep inside resides the ego, selfishness, this love of ourselves which began the day that the first-created fell. This was the great evil that happened on that day – the first-created stopped looking to God and began looking to themselves. They turned toward themselves. And so all the dreadful things begin from that point on and reach all the way to today. And while we're baptized and we should be living differently somehow, in the end we don't manage to live in a genuinely Christian way but instead we live erroneously. Perhaps also the period the times we live in favor such unhealthy situations.

Let's pray that what we're saying will help us a little, especially now that we're in this period, so that this year the idealized image we have inside us may finally be crucified. Let's say, "Let's fall, in some way, either from out of the airplane or from anywhere else – as long as we get our ego crucified, together with Christ, of course, and our self resurrected together with the Lord."

The Idealized Image Must Die

Our topic is the idealized image, which we've talked about so much this year.

This idealized image must die. If the idealized image within us doesn't die, there's no point in talking about the Cross, about Christ's passion, there's no point in believing that we're celebrating Holy Week, the Crucifixion and the Resurrection of Christ, because within us lives a wild beast which ought to and should die.[1]

In our previous talk we were saying that the idealized image reaches the point of deceiving us. For example, at the moment that we trust some person, at the moment we see him as holy and believe in him and follow him as a saint and base our existence on him in a way, the idealized image deceives us. Because this person can be an ordinary person. Certainly he can be something, have something, but not have any of the type of holiness we think he does. We, however, can't see this, we can't recognize it.

How often do some souls wonder, "How could I not recognize that? How could I not see that? How did I get led astray?" You were led astray, you didn't realize, you closed your eyes, because you transferred your own idealized image to this person. Since your self couldn't stand for you to have inside you this fearsome idealized image, since you couldn't reconcile these things well enough – that is, this fearful idealized image you have and what you are in reality – for this reason you put this idealized image onto this person. And now you see him precisely as this image you have fashioned shows him to you and not as he himself is in reality, and you're attached to him and rely on him in a way

---

1   This talk took place shortly before Holy Week and the speaker made reference to it at the beginning.

that's harmful for you and for him.

It alienates us from our real self

The idealized image does something even worse – it alienates the person from himself. That is, as one identifies with the idealized image, he ceases to be with his real self and puts himself into contact with an imaginary self, with a fictitious self. For this reason he reaches the point of not quite understanding what's happening to him, of not understanding what he feels, what he wants, what he seeks, and what he's aiming at.

There are more than a few souls that suffer something of the sort. In fact, they even come to the point of not having any interest in life. While they have been alienated from their real self – in the meantime they still encounter reality on a daily basis in life – they don't have any interest in life, they can't even make decisions and do this or that.

And what's still worse is that as things deteriorate in their lives, they come to the point of having a condition created inside them as if they are in a state of non-existence. That is, it's as if they don't exist, and as if this person that lives and does this and that – their self – is someone else. It's a terrible situation, and unfortunately quite a few souls come to this point and have a great deal of difficulty.

A sick person once used to say, "I'd be wonderful, I'd get by just great, I'd be in terrific shape if it weren't for reality." Reality, it seems, causes the person constantly to find himself in a conflict. So if daily reality didn't exist in life this person would feel just great. And this happens precisely because he's living in the clouds.

When we can't stand ourselves as we are…

Something else. The person who fashions an idealized image does it solely because he can't stand himself as he is. That is, he can't agree with his real self, he can't co-exist with it.

A person may begin to suffer something of the sort as a small child. He sees himself as he is in reality, and it wears him out. He's not just worn out – he can't stand himself. He can't bear himself as he is, and he creates the idealized image. But when someone fashions an idealized image and identifies with it, he certainly may have forgotten himself, and yet his self continues to exist right alongside this idealized image.

What does this mean? This means that from that lowly point where his self was – as he saw his reality – now in some way, he sees it at a high place, where he has his idealized image. And you understand what is being created. Where he wanted to trample himself down, now he admires himself loftily. And a fearful struggle is created, a conflict. Because yes, on the one hand he is in the grip of the idealized image, but there alongside the idealized image he also sees his filthy self – as perhaps he would be so bold as to characterize it – that self that he dislikes, that he doesn't want, that he can't stand, but he sees it and there it is.

What happens now? That's where the big drama begins. On the one hand he worships himself because he identifies with the idealized image. On the other hand, however, he sees what a mess he is and he lives with a constant self-contempt, with a constant condemnation of himself, complaining for no reason at all. And some people think that this – self-contempt, condemnation of themselves – is Christian, that it's a virtue. Sometimes, in fact, as they see something of the sort in the Fathers, they think that they're living exactly like the Fathers. It's not like that, however. Not even for a minute did the Fathers let themselves depart from reality. Their real self never escaped from their eyes, and not even for a minute did they let themselves pass over into an idealized image.

So the thought of the Fathers is a different thing, their mentality is different, their souls move and operate differently. We simply take a few of their phrases in order to justify our own ugly situation.

A dictatorship inside the person

One sees certain souls living in agony, on the one hand, to hold onto this idealized image, and on the other hand living a torment as they see themselves, their real selves, having one thing and another and yet another – all the passions, all the shortcomings, all those things that the soul can't stand and can't bear to see, and yet one drags them along in oneself. And so in the end a terrible conflict gets created inside the person.

On the one hand there are the initial desires, the initial tendencies, which aren't always in one specific direction but can be in different directions, the tendencies which create the initial conflict and cause the person to create the idealized image. On the other hand, precisely because this conflict occurs between the idealized image and our real self, a sort of dictatorship is created inside the person and we don't realize it.

Karen Horney, who has occupied herself particularly with these topics, says that the same thing happens in this dictatorship as in political dictatorships. There, either one identifies with the dictatorship or tries to reach that point where one will become agreeable or become a revolutionary.

Similarly here. Either one identifies with this dictatorship that the idealized image creates within him, where the person becomes narcissistic – he worships himself, he's self-satisfied, he's pleased with himself – or he lives with a continual activity, with a continual effort, unhealthy however – with a panting, with an anguish that doesn't leave him in peace – in order to reach up to this idealized image that he has fashioned, or he finds himself in a state of revolution. That is, as he sees the idealized image he has enthroned inside himself, he revolts against it continuously – don't let this surprise you – but the idealized image is now well enthroned.

Let me add that in someone who has an idealized image, all three of the above stances can appear before it. In another person two may appear, and in yet another person only one. Don't let this surprise us. There are souls who for a period of time don't sleep, don't find peace, don't rest, attend one sermon after another, if you want me to put it like that – they will go to all the sermons and to whatever other functions take place – and they also submit themselves, they attach themselves in order to reach perfection, as they are entranced by the idealized image. They don't make any progress at all, however, in a regular and correct way. And as soon as they see that what they pursued isn't achieved, they change stance before the idealized image. They revolt and oppose it. And you'll see them, where they weren't sleeping at all, now they don't wake up at all. Where they used to be most strict with regard to ethics, with regard to fasting, with regard to obedience, with regard to going to church and with regard to other questions, now they take the completely opposite stance, as if they want in some way to revenge themselves on the idealized image. And so we may have a person one time take one stance before the idealized image, and another time the other, and the only thing that he doesn't do is to take the correct stance.

An obstacle in the spiritual life

All these things we've spoken about up till now are like a wall that prevents the person from progressing smoothly and having a smooth development and real progress in the spiritual life. After all, the person who is overcome and identified with the idealized image keeps trying in some way to reach some good spiritual condition and absolutely never succeeds in anything because there is this wall that doesn't let him have any progress.

What one needs, then, is to pay special attention and to become aware of this fictitious, imaginary, idealized image he has fashioned. And he needs to search here, to search there, to see it in one of its details, to see it in another of its details, and to understand very clearly that when he has this image and as long as he has this image, all his labors, all his efforts for spiritual progress and all his sleeplessness are going to waste.

Unfortunately a person doesn't understand this easily. He makes so many mistakes and doesn't see them, doesn't recognize them since they're wrapped up with the idealized image. Consequently he can't move forward. However, when one understands this, that everything is wasted while he has the idealized image inside him, perhaps he may decide, certainly with the help of God's grace – in regards to us Christians – to put this image to death.

We want to be Christians but without dying on Christ's cross

We spoke at the beginning about the death and the Cross of Christ. We have to say that we suffer all these things because we don't want to be crucified with Christ. We suffer all these things because, as we were saying at another time, we want to be Christians but without dying on the Cross of Christ together with Christ in order to proceed to the Resurrection. We want to be Christians and at the same time to be as we came out from Adam. That doesn't work.

We should stop being children of Adam. From now on let's be children of Christ. And one becomes a child of Christ when he dies in relation to his former condition. That is, when in Christ Jesus he stops being a child of Adam, then he becomes a child of Christ. But again for this to happen, that is, for the idealized image to be put to death, isn't something easy. It's easy for someone to take a knife and cut something, but in this case things aren't so easy.

One must be able to understand where he started out from, where the creation of this idealized image began. And if we think matters over, if we examine them closely, we'll see that perhaps it began already in our childhood years. Certainly we get baptized, when we are small children, but what happens from that point on? Either because our parents or our priests didn't pay attention to us, or because society is the way it is, and so we don't live in the midst of a genuine Christian environment, or because the evil one is keeping watch within us or for other reasons, since our childhood, one person in this way and another in that way, we avoid this death.

This death is brought about in baptism. But in baptism something can happen that's analogous with what happens when a tree is grafted. The wild tree that's grafted can become domesticated, a new tree, but, if one leaves it alone, the wild tree can revive from the old root. That is, a bunch of shoots can sprout from it and the graft, the little domesticated twig that was placed to graft the tree, barely survives. In a similar way if a Christian doesn't live in conformity with baptism, he'll be as if he didn't die along with Christ during his baptism, and the old man will be revived.

One needs, then, by a return, by repentance, by humility, by all the others means and by the mysteries, to die as the old man and to die continuously, to live continuously the death of Christ in order also to live Christ's Resurrection. If we do this, we'll feel pain just once – if I may say this – and it'll be over. But if we don't do it this way and we avoid this death or permit what should be dead within us to revive, then we'll be in pain continuously, we'll suffer continuously, unsolvable problems will be created continuously without any progress. While, when one identifies himself with Christ, when he's crucified with Christ and suffers together with Christ and remains in this death, he remains in this passion of Christ's, he suffers once, he dies once, he's crucified together with Christ one time. One time but forever, that is, for his whole life.

And certainly a person doesn't become a saint immediately, he doesn't become perfect immediately, he doesn't reach the end of the path immediately, he doesn't become immediately – the same day, the same year – what the Lord told us: "You must be perfect, as your heavenly Father is perfect."[2] But he's on the path – today a little, tomorrow some more, the next day a little more. And he makes progress.

…and as for us, we are at the point of being ashamed!

Once more, please, let's think whether we happen not to have taken the path correctly, whether we happen not to be thinking correctly, whether we happen not to be Christians in the correct and genuine way while we think we are, and

---

2 Matthew 5: 48.

whether in the end we'll be "of all men most to be pitied,"³ the most miserable of all people, as the Apostle Paul says.

We have already come to believe in Christ. We have already come to know Him. Let's undertake a reexamination. Let's take another look at things – whether we happen to have been led astray – in order to find the correct path. So many, way ahead of us, have truly taken the path and have reached the end, while as for us, we're at the point of being ashamed! Both before ourselves and before the world in which we live and should give witness, we're at the point of being ashamed.

Who can affirm, first to himself and then by using the reality of his existence, persuade others, too, that he has really found the truth, that he has found holiness, that he has found the Spirit of God? That he has really found what every person should find and accept in order to become a true person and be saved?

We're near the point of changing our minds about being Christians. We're near the point of beginning to doubt internally: "Could it be that we aren't doing well? Could it be that we've been led astray? Could it be that others have the truth?" That is, whether those who don't believe are doing better, those who don't pay attention to God? This is frightful, but it's a reality. I think I am not far off the mark when I say this and emphasize it.

The Church isn't afraid. A Christian shouldn't be afraid. If the Church as a whole and Christians – each of us separately – live the Cross of Christ and have within us this life that Christ gives to each one who dies together with

---

3 See 1 Corinthians 15: 19.

Him, and if we have nothing else, neither shall we worry or complain or weep about it nor shall we change our minds about following Christ. But the fact that we have something within us that others don't have, these others will see that we have it. And this will be the witness that we'll give to the contemporary world as the Church. And whoever of those happens to be of good disposition and good intentions will believe and will themselves become followers of Christ.

Certainly whoever wants to believe will believe. The ones who don't want to, don't want to. Christ hasn't brought anyone to His side by violence. Who are we to bring them in that way?

The Externalization of the Idealized Image[1]

Consequences from the void and the conflict

Based on what we've said up to now, we understand that an unbridgeable gap is created between the idealized image that each person fashions for himself and his real self.

Of course a person fashions the idealized image in order to avoid the conflicts that torment him, but then the conflict between the idealized image and the real self is even greater and so the person tries to find different solutions.

And as we explained in previous talks, the person sometimes does this, sometimes that, but he ends up getting more confused. And all this happens because he's tightly connected with the idealized image which is everything to him. Consequently it's as if he's destroying his very self if he wants to remove his idealized image, and that's why he doesn't do it. And so the idealized image continues to remain and have the results that we've mentioned. In any case, as the idealized image exists, but our real self also exists, and as a gap is created between the idealized image and our real self and this gap and consequently this conflict continues to exist, the person doesn't find peace and rest. He's not satisfied, but he keeps grumbling, in a way, to himself and to others.

According to psychologists, another solution the person has recourse to as he lives out this conflict between himself – his real self – and the idealized image, is externalization or projection.

In the past we've said quite a bit about projection. Now we need to say a few things again in relation to the idealized

---

[1] In this and the following talk the references to the book *Our Inner Conflicts* refer to the chapter on externalization, pp. 115-30.

image, in relation to this conflict that's created between the idealized image and our real self.

No matter how much the person fashions an idealized image inside him and identifies with it, he can't be unaware of his real self. His real self exists. That's the one which has passions, shortcomings, deficiencies, weaknesses, which has all the badness inside it. And since this reality exists, it gets expressed. As much as a person wants to idealize things, as much as he wants to disguise them, this reality exists. Therefore whether he wants to or not, he'll be dejected and disturbed. Whether he wants to or not, he'll get angry, whether he wants to or not, he'll always be annoyed by something. For as long as he doesn't decide to cast away the idealized image and on the other hand his real self exists, the gap exists inside him, the conflict exists, the ugly situation exists. What's going to happen?

Without fully realizing it, then, one begins to externalize his self and project it onto others. That is, he stops seeing in himself his various shortcomings or the various difficult conditions he has inside him, or – to put it better – he stops attributing them to himself and begins to see them in some way in others who are outside himself. The result is that in this way the person distances himself from his own self.

It's said, in fact, that the matter reaches such a state that often those who protest about small countries that are oppressed – they organize rallies, send telegrams, make demonstrations, write, speak on the radio, and so forth – do all these things because there is a commensurate condition inside them. Given that with externalization, with someone's projecting himself onto others, he doesn't merely project certain shortcomings, he doesn't merely externalize and cast certain errors upon the other, but in some way he projects his whole being and his emotions.

A person who isn't free inside, then, one who is bound up with various passions and feels a weight inside him and is oppressed by this weight, in order for him to be unburdened a little, to be alleviated a little from this condition in which he finds himself, in some way, he locates something analogous that exists in others. For example, one reaches the point while he's the one who's angry at himself or others, he thinks that others are angry with him. Or again he can reach the point, as we said, of protesting supposedly about countries that are oppressed by other countries.

Victims without realizing it

This ugly condition can take on still greater dimensions and if a person isn't paying attention, he will be a victim of it. That is, for example, one may take care of a prisoner, a poor person, a hungry person, any sort of needy person, whoever happens to be in need. And not only take care of them, but one may not even have time to sleep since he's occupied with this work. And one may even use his time set aside for sleep and move heaven and earth and go about over land and sea for a task of this sort.[2] And it's possible that he does all these things because deep inside he's sick, because deep inside him he's oppressed. Just as he has the idealized image and is identified with it, he's oppressed by his real self, which causes him to feel that he's in prison, that he's hungry, it causes him to feel that he's miserable, that he finds himself in some sort of need. In which case he externalizes this by taking care of people who are hungry, who are in prison, and so forth. We need to pay a great deal of attention, then. The question isn't what one is doing, as we've said at other times. The question is why one is doing it.

---

2 See Matthew 23: 15.

Certainly when we do a good thing, the good thing is good. It doesn't cease to be good in itself. God certainly knows how good it is. But we, though, who do this good thing, when we don't do it motivated by love, by virtue, when we don't do it out of altruism – if you want to put it that way – and for the glory of God, but we do it prompted by unhealthy motivations, by an unnatural inner need, then we find ourselves in a very ugly condition and we're victims, regardless of whether or not this condition of ours is supposedly expressed as virtue. In reality we're victims of an unhealthy condition, of a conflict that exists between the idealized image and our real self.

This is the reason that the Fathers – who knew these things better than us – didn't allow anyone all that easily to begin to do a task for other human beings – certainly we are talking about one who would consult them, who would ask them, who would want their guidance. According to the Fathers and as we know very well, the first and foremost thing for every soul is to be cleansed, to be humbled, to become spirit-bearing. The soul needs to learn to subject itself to God, to learn really to love God and human beings, to learn to work for the glory of God and not work compulsively, to serve an inner need.

Some people don't have any peace, in a way, unless they're taking care of others. But this matter of "not having any peace," does it possibly originate from a lot of holiness, from a lot of virtue, does it come perhaps, from the great love they have for God, does it really come from a disposition for God's name to be glorified? Or is it perhaps an inner need to settle the conflict that exists inside them and for the person somehow to let off steam, and consequently for the sake of an illness, for the sake of a weakness, in the final analysis does it happen for the sake of a sinful condition?

You see, then, how many things the old man can create inside us and how much we can be its victims without realizing it.

Consequently the person who reaches such a point of engaging in what we called externalization or projection – it's clear that he always defines his life in relation to others. We'd say that his life is influenced by others. His inner attitude in general and all his movement and all his expressions depend on others. That is, a person can have a good disposition if others, too, have a good disposition with him. Or it can be that he doesn't feel well precisely because others don't feel well with him. The matter gets to that point.

There are many such souls which have peace, calm, joy, happiness within them when others smile at them and in general when others are found in a good relationship with them. But when others happen to grind their teeth, when they make long faces, just because they are who they are, then it ruins their mood and it overturns all the external peace they had.

This can't be Christian life. This can't happen in a normal, natural person. This happens only in a person who isn't settled inside and he projects all his conflicts and all his ugly condition onto others and as a result he depends psychologically on others.

Psychological emptiness

Let's add something more and finish with this topic. This externalization, this projection reaches such a point that when someone takes such a stance and expresses himself in some such manner, he depends so much on others that as a rule, an emptiness is created within him.

When we talk about externalization or projection, we mean, as we said, that the very thing which someone is inside himself, he lays on, he sets down to the account of others, he attributes it to others; he thinks that this bad thing inside him is inside others. Externalization, then, reaches such a point that an emptiness is created inside the person. And this emptiness is expressed most often as a feeling of an empty stomach, and that's why one may eat more and more, to fill his stomach. Don't be surprised when you discover sometimes that you have – I may say – an unjustified gluttony.

One watches his weight, he weighs too much, but in spite of this he eats a little here, a little there, a little of one thing, a little of another, it's like there's something empty inside him and he has to fill it to become somewhat more normal, more natural, somewhat more relaxed and calm. The emptiness that exists inside him is much more psychological; it isn't physiological. In spite of all that one tries to fill this psychological emptiness with such things.

Take a look and you'll see that very often one eats pointlessly. Very often one feels that something is missing and that's why he wants to eat. The same thing happens more generally when someone always wants to hear something, wants to learn something, supposedly wants to see something. It's that emptiness more generally which exists inside him which causes him to express himself in this way.

Something of the sort can also happen with regard to the question of money. A great many people, we would say, have not given their soul to money nor do they want to have a lot of money in order to spend it and have a good time. Another sort of people are the pleasure-seekers, those who want to have a lot of money to spend. But the ones we're talking about don't have a disposition of that sort. In spite of that, however, there's a tendency within them to get a little money from here, a little from there, to secure a little from here, a little from there so as to fill a psychological emptiness that exists within them. And they think that it will fill up in this way.

The person who will begin to be reborn sees with another pair of eyes

So as to put this topic to rest for now, let me say this. Please, let's pay a little more attention. This idealized image is a great deal of trouble and it creates ugly situations for us.

Of course there's no room for doubt that all these things have their start and are cultivated, nourished, exist and remain by reason of the fact that the person doesn't humble himself, doesn't make a decision to give himself to God and trust in Him completely. And that's why he's gripped and seized by the idealized image.

Someone, as we said, may fashion a more exaggerated image, and another may fashion one perhaps a little more humbly. In any case, each one fashions something imaginary, but it does not change the fact that in reality each person is what he is deep down. We're obstinate and conceited and neurotic, we're quick-tempered and ambitious, and we're cunning.

However much one refuses to see these things in himself, he does see them in some way and then the fearsome conflict is created between the idealized image and this reality. And then what happens? Then the person himself begins to see these things that he has in others. Do you know how many of the things we see in others are in us?

You must have all noticed that when we have a spiritual euphoria within us, when God's grace has visited our soul somewhat, when our existence is found in a somewhat humble condition, it's as if we're seeing with another pair of eyes. Not merely the sea, the mountains, the trees, the birds, but people themselves who up to a short time ago we hated and were inclined to take vengeance on because we thought they were our enemies and that they were ready to pounce on us, now we see them from a new condition that has been created within us and consequently we see them differently.

This is the reason the Fathers say – you are probably aware of it – that the humble person, the repentant person, the person who has been visited by God's grace, he who little by little will begin to enter God's path and begin little by little to be reborn, he sees all people as saints, because in fact he sees with another pair of eyes. This happens because this person projects – in the good sense now – his own inner world onto others.

While, on the contrary, the person who flounders about between the idealized image and his real self – and he's a victim of this condition – constantly projects his ugly self onto others and he sees all his own shortcomings in others. How can this person then find peace and how can he come into good relations with others, communicate with them, work with them and do something worthwhile? When we say "with others" we don't mean distant people, unknown people. We mean the mother having a good relationship with her child, the brother with his sister and his brother, the father with his children. But how many times does one person weigh down on the other!

How much more peaceful, calmer our life would be, how much truer our life would be, if we were somewhat released from the conflict that is created between the idealized image and our real self, which causes us to externalize and project our self – our shortcomings and whatever we have inside us – onto others. If we were released from this conflict, our life would really be a lot better.

Self-Contempt[1]

Something we live without realizing it

We have been talking about the idealized image and more particularly about the distance, the chasm that exists between the idealized image and our real self. And we've been saying that because of this distance that exists between them, an externalization is created, a projection, as a reaction. That is, a person externalizes a situation that exists inside him and projects it onto others.

The more the person – that is, the person's ego, our being – identifies with the idealized image – and consequently our being is far from our real self, and in this way there is this gap – the more this whole situation is unconscious within us. That is, we are oblivious to the fact that it's happening like this. We have no idea. It's not just that we don't realize it, but we don't even suspect it.

And of course our self reacts from out of the unconscious and it reacts in an unconscious manner – that is, without our understanding it. This unconscious reaction – says Karen Horney, who, as I've told you, appears to be the best among the great psychologists – is expressed, among other ways, either with self-contempt or in anger or in a feeling of inner pressure. That is, this ugly condition that exists within us is projected outwards, it's externalized in these ways. (She certainly explains these things from a clearly psychological standpoint. We'd also say something similar, however, from the spiritual standpoint. To be sure we must emphasize that all these things aren't merely painful, but they render the person incapable of living.)

---

[1] See p. 167 footnote 1.

Self-contempt can be expressed either by contempt for others or by contempt for oneself. This depends on the person, on who this person is.

Remember that when we referred to the types of people, we said that there are the aggressive type, the compliant type, and the type that isolates himself. An aggressive type will always express his contempt for himself on others. That is, he'll have contempt for others. When a person has contempt for others, deep down he has contempt for himself. The compliant type feels rather that he's being looked down on by others. If spiritual X-rays existed to show us what each of us is, what chaos would we see existing inside us!

The more one has cultivated an idealized image and is in the grip of it and identified with it, the more he has contempt for himself, because his real self exists, and, whether he wants to or not, this reality of himself is expressed. In which case subconsciously, unconsciously, in any case without realizing it, he feels contempt for himself. But he just lives this without realizing that he lives it. And how is it expressed? It's expressed, as was said, by loathing others or by feeling that others look down on him. To be sure, when one feels that he's being looked down on by others, we'd say it's worse, even though it appears to be better.

And of course this contempt is something ugly. It isn't the contempt the saints and ascetics talk about. Here, in the way the saints live and teach, there exists our real self, which is sinful, and the person must look to holy God and his sinful self and humble himself. For example, the ascetic who strikes himself down as a fisherman beats an octopus on a rock to tenderize it, on the one hand sees his self humbly, but on the other hand with clear eyes he sees the holiness of God, the grandeur of God, and he really lives in that dimension. On the one hand he sees holy God and on the other hand he sees his wretched being. As St. Nikodemos the Hagiorite says, on the one hand the person must completely lose hope in himself, and on the other hand he must hope completely in God if he wants to be saved.[2] Otherwise he can't be saved. This is a genuine life-altering experience.

Beyond this genuine situation, however, there's another reality. In our days contemporary man – and also he who considers himself a good Christian – has perverted this genuine thing, he has distorted it. On account of his egoism, his pride, his presumption, his hypocrisy – on account of the fact that we live in a false way in life – he has fashioned an idealized image about himself. He's in the grip, then, of this idealized image which is a fabrication of his imagination – and it's satanic pride – and since he wants to be the idealized image, he identifies himself with it. In the meantime there exists his real self and deep down he lives that, which in reality is his self. So without realizing it he takes a negative, loathing position toward himself, but out of egoism and not out of real humility. He has contempt for himself in an unhealthy way, that is, egoistically, arrogantly. And this is expressed – although he himself certainly doesn't realize it – either by contempt for others or by thinking that others express contempt for him.

And we've emphasized that this second thing is even worse because it makes the person timid, fearful, it causes helplessness, it causes the person to isolate himself and become a victim of haughty and egoistic people who exist in this society, and of course it causes him a great deal of suffering.

---

2 See *Unseen Warfare* (*The Spiritual Combat & Path to Paradise* of Lorenzo Scupoli ed. by Nicodemus of the Holy Mountain and revised by Theophan the Recluse). St. Vladimir's Seminary Press. Crestwood, NY, 1987. tr. E. Kadloubovsky and G. E. H. Palmer. pp. 78-9; 81-7.

When our wretched being is suddenly unmasked…

But the worst thing of all for this person – in whom this ugly inner condition is created on account of the gap between the idealized image and his real self and is expressed as self-contempt – the ugliest thing is for his whole wretched being to be suddenly unmasked and for him in some way to stop seeing his idealized image which supports him a little in life, to see himself naked, where there is the most wretched image that exists; the other extreme – in relation to the idealized image – that exists inside him. That is, when abruptly and suddenly he sees this, then the person collapses, he's literally shattered, he loses hope, he becomes discouraged. In a certain way he doesn't find anything inside him that he can rely on in order to stand a little on his own feet and take a little courage, make a little effort so as to be able to make a prayer to God. Where can one find the disposition for such things! Where can one find the effort!

And this, you know, is something that happens quite often today in this society where we live. Quite a few people, from a position where they live and flourish among us, from a position where they know all the tricks, from a position where they are presented as being very solid, that they know a lot, and they say a lot, suddenly they collapse, precisely because their real self is unmasked before their eyes and this idealized image vanishes completely. How does a multi-story building tumble down and nothing remains standing? That's how they collapse.

Truth comes by itself to man. It's not found by man. Salvation comes by itself to man. It's not found by man. Sanctification come by itself to man. God gives it. It's not found by man himself.

Let go of the idealized images and repent sincerely before God. Really humble yourself and look at the little thing you are. Rely on it and ask your Heavenly Father to give you the great thing.

The weakest, the most sinful human being – when he decides to let himself go to God's grace – he'll be redeemed.

In Place of an Epilogue

As we gain understanding from everything that has been said in this book, each of us is helped to know himself better. However, the cure of the soul from the various unhealthy conditions – not only from those discussed here but also from others – isn't so much a matter of the science of psychology. For us Orthodox Christians the question within the Church is crystal-clear.

There are two basic things each of us must have in view. One is that we need to be obedient within the Church. The second is that we need to see what's happening to us in the whole work of God's economy for our salvation. In this way we'll become receptive to God's grace, which in fact heals man from both psychological and spiritual illnesses.

We considered it beneficial to quote a few extracts from the book published by us, *...All Things Work for Good*, where what we're saying above appears clearly. These extracts are only a little example of the lecturer's positions on these topics, which we also discussed in the introductory note.

Obedience in the Church

In our days whoever wants to save his soul must be obedient. Although what we're saying isn't absolute, this is still the rule. I don't know if a person can be saved without obedience. If, then, each of us must be obedient, this holds still more for those who have unhealthy conditions.

If one is obedient – truly obedient, that is – he'll escape slowly from the gears in which he's enmeshed – from the various unhealthy conditions, from the various complexes – he'll move more comfortably and will be delivered.

I think I already told you at another gathering – it could be that I am making a mistake, I could be falling into error, and I take back my words from those who would not accept them – that I've noticed that those who up to now have listened to me and trusted me were not mistaken. It has turned out very well. We have circumstances in which we've gotten to know someone and worked with him about his soul for a year, two years, three years, and as he was extremely obedient and showed tremendous trust, a great deal of good came about for his soul.

If it's necessary for each person to be obedient, it's all the more important for the unhealthy type. And we have to say that people today, and especially the youth, have terrible psychological problems, even when that doesn't appear to be the case.

People today are so dominated by their own selves, by the whole sinful and unhealthy condition they have inside them – since sin and sickness go hand in hand – they're so tangled up, so enslaved, that only obedience can save them. In particular, all this entanglement of the soul with sin and with the unhealthy condition is due – even if this doesn't always appear to be the case – to the fact that deep down there's an acquiescence of the soul. And this can't remain in obedience. It'll go away. No matter how it goes, if one holds onto obedience, this acquiescence will go away. The question is for one to endure obedience, to make a decision to be obedient and to endure it to the end.

Man is selfish, he's egocentric. We don't understand it, we have no idea, but we sink into it the way psychopaths sink into their illness.

A love has been built up, an entanglement – and we don't get disentangled easily – with the worship of ourselves, with the care for ourselves, with selfishness. This is expressed sometimes as a fear that we'll suffer something, as an insecurity, an isolation, an uneasiness – that things in life won't go well, that I won't succeed, that I'll make a mistake, that they'll deceive me – and what will I do? At other times it's expressed as a worry that I'll lose this or that, that I won't have time for this, that I won't have time for the other. At other times again it's expressed as a desire to take pleasure in this thing, to enjoy that other thing. And all these things are vanity. From one point of view all these things are created, and one lives them in this way because we embrace the wretched ego. As soon as one is set free of the ego, they disappear.

I told you last time and I'm emphasizing it again now, that this appears especially in psychopaths. But we would dare to say that from one point of view all men are psychopaths. That is, from one point of view. And there are those circumstances that are striking, and that help us see what's happening to all of us. In these circumstances the effective thing is delivered, the *coup de grace* – and the road is opened, and things move forward – if one is obedient.

I was saying in a particular circumstance these days: "My child, the way things are now, you already have some experience. You made a mess of it. Enough. You acted in this way, you acted in that way, you made this effort and you made that effort. The only thing that happened was that you made more of a mess, like a bug entangling itself when it falls into a spider's web and the poor thing supposedly wants to get away, but the harder it tries to escape the more it gets wrapped up in it. Since you are where you are," I told him, "what harm is there in your saying, 'I made a mess of it. I came to this father. Coming to him shows that I have a certain trust in him. So I'll do what he tells me.' For a period of time at least. They aren't going to impose anything on you and you have nothing to lose." But he doesn't do it. He doesn't do it and he's tormented. Experience showed solidly, in an absolute way, that whoever wants to believe in what they tell him – certainly with the presupposition that he can have trust, and while from his own point of view he doesn't see any progress, but just makes a mess – he's set free.

In God's economy for our salvation

There are circumstances where someone has a bad character, if I may use that term. Someone will say immediately: "Why does God allow me to have such a character and to struggle?" He can't accept this easily and it causes a great harm in the soul, in the sense that he feels as if God is wronging him. Apart from that, there is a mechanism of self-defense in man's soul, through which in the end one enters into alliance with his character, defends it, and in practice – perhaps not theoretically – he tries in this way and that to prove that his character is good.

And here things get complicated. Here what's needed is for him to humble himself and say, "It appears that I wouldn't be saved if I had a purer and better character."

Because salvation isn't a question of character.

Adam was a saint when he was in paradise, but that didn't save him. Man isn't saved simply by a good character. There are certain men who are by nature of good character, but this isn't enough for someone to be saved. In society, certainly, in relationship with other people one can appear good, but this isn't salvation.

The other person on the other hand suffers with his bad character. And what he must do, I repeat, is to humble himself and to say, "God allowed it because if I had a good character, who knows what arrogance would have taken hold of me? While now, as I am what I am whether I like it or not, I'm humbling myself. How can I be arrogant?" If one sees it correctly, then, he humbles himself, he humbles himself and thanks God: "My God, what a bad thing, what a misfortune I thought my bad character was for me. I had been asking myself what I would do with such a character, and now I see that this was salvation for me. I thank You, my God, I'm grateful to You."

God loves us. And as God Who loves each of us, He showed economy, He allowed things to come upon you in this way out of love. Believe that. That is, believe – but believe it now – that in the end whatever happens to you will be for your own benefit.

Stop and think about the fact that your soul wouldn't have been saved if God didn't manage things with such economy that you were caught in the snare where you find yourself trapped. Your soul wouldn't be saved otherwise. If one studies this well enough, if one sees it well enough, he'll find a lot of material to become aware of his sin before God and humble himself to feel the potential arrogance his soul has, the potential rebellion his soul has, the potential opposition he has within him before God. And that's why God had to show His economy in things in this way, so as to nail him down. Because if He hadn't nailed him down, who knows what he would have done?

It's enough for one just to think like this, and immediately he'll collapse and say, "My God, is there any other sinner like me?" It's certainly possible for him to be overcome by a grievance: "Why did this happen to me?" But if he gets past that, he'll say, "My God, while I am who I am, while I was going to do those things I was going to do, in spite of all that You loved me and You found a way to grab me and bind me and to save me in the end." This is certainly something that costs him.

If one studies the truths we're saying now, he'll find that all the negative things in his life are God's blessings. All the negative things. Certainly this is not to say that these things considered by themselves are blessings of God. The fact that you have within you a condition that has the potential to do who knows what against God is a bad thing. Who knows what would come of this and that and the other thing you have within you? All these things are ugly, by themselves they're bad, but all the same, as God manages His economy, they're blessings because God took all these things – mistakes, passions, weaknesses, unhealthy conditions – which are your own, and He managed them with such a manner of economy, He put them into His plan in such a way that in the end you can become a saint.

Are you grateful to God or not for whatever difficulty you have, for whatever weakness, for whatever shortcoming you have? In this way one moves into a completely different condition. He doesn't lament over his fate, as many people do – those who have such burdens within them and they weep in a way for their fate, why this?, why that? – but he begins to be grateful to God, to thank God and glorify Him. And he already begins to enjoy all that love that God shows him in that special providence He provided for him – that is, that He allowed for him to have all these ugly conditions to lead him, in the end, to salvation.

While these things appear to be very frightful, all the same, as we talk about them in this way, in the end, if you believe me, if you understand me, I feel – but perhaps I'm making a mistake – it's as if I'm lifting some unbearable burdens off you, and you'll leave here with wings if there's really humility in your soul. Otherwise, that is, if ones leaves here with wings but without humility in him, he'll be conceited.

Do you feel that way?